Hope you enjoy the story!
Barb Bland

RUNNING

FREE

RUNNING FREE

The Memoir of a Dog Rescuer

By Barb Bland

ISBN: 1490966811
ISBN 13: 9781490966816
LCCN: 2013913669
CreateSpace Independent Publishing Platform, North Charleston, SC

Credits

Maps:
Washington State/Whidbey Island map on page 7 is drawn by the author.
Fort Ebey State Park map on page 151 is reprinted by permission of Steve Ford, Trax Maps, PO Box 817, Langley, WA 98260. Copyright 1997 Trax Maps.

Photographs:
The "Pets of the Week" photo on page 38 is reprinted with permission of the *Whidbey News-Times*.
Sweetie Gonzalez on page 17 is reprinted with permission of Island County Animal Control Officer Carol Barnes.
Shy Pikachu on page 92 is by Ron Kerrigan.
Piki, Blue, and Barb on page 175 is by Curt Bland.
Blue and Piki on page 187 is by Jen Wigg.
Piki on page 227 is by the Stadler Studio of Photography, Langley, WA.
Hand on Head on page 249 is by Rhia Drouillard.
Barb Bland on page 265 is by Avalee Harmon.

All other photographs, including the cover photo, the "Lost Dog Poster" on page 137, and the drawing on page 91 are by the author.

Book:
William R. Koehler, *The Koehler Method of Dog Training, Certified Techniques by Movieland's Most Experienced Dog Trainer*, Howell Book House, Macmillan Publishing Company, New York, 1962.

Printed by CreateSpace

For WAIF
(Whidbey Animals' Improvement Foundation)
and specifically for

Pam Lock,
who had the idea to create WAIF
and got it off the ground

Shari Bibich,
whose dedication as shelter manager
made WAIF a success

Pikachu,
the WAIF dog
who saved my life in return

A Note on the Text

Though the story itself is factual, the names of most of the people and some of the dogs have been changed.

In most books dealing with animals, the pronoun used to describe those with four legs is *it*. Because I regard animals as peers, as friends, and in some cases as members of my immediate family—I also view them as gender-specific individuals with personalities and preferences, with intellects and emotions, and the pronouns I use for animals are *he* and *she*, *his* and *her*. Anything less would be inaccurate.

Animals are not objects. It is the very point of this book.

Contents

Part One

The Pokémon Puppies and WAIF

1.

The Beginning

April 2000

"I'm tired of taking care of them." The young man struggled through the front door of the animal shelter, carrying a large cardboard box. He set the box on the floor and kicked it toward the reception desk. "I asked you to take 'em when they were born."

I had just come in from the kennels, and the first thing I noticed was that everything about this young man was dark: the color of his hair, the scowl on his face, the belligerence in his voice. From where I stood, I could see activity inside that box. It bumped and shook, and when the angry young man bent over and opened a corner of the lid, the eight black, squirming puppies inside started working to push the lid completely open. It took them less than a minute.

The man turned to leave, but Patty, the shelter employee sitting at the desk, jumped up to intercept him. She handed him the paperwork necessary to legally surrender the dogs. A formality. He scrawled the minimum of information: Labrador Retriever-Border Collie mixes, three months old, the date, his name, a South Whidbey address. And then he left, slamming the door behind him.

"This was the guy who phoned yesterday," Patty said. The two of us knelt to look at the lively puppies trying to get out of their box. "He threatened to shoot them all if WAIF didn't take them now." She said he had called early in the new year, wanting to surrender the puppies almost immediately after their birth. Shelter personnel had talked him out of separating the puppies from their mother until they were at least weaned.

Patty started to enter their information into the computer: four males and four females. "Can you come up with eight names?" she asked me. Whenever it was possible, this was our practice: naming puppies from a single litter in a way that would show their relationship.

I thought for a moment. "The Seven Dwarfs plus one?"

I was kidding, but Patty said, "Already been used."

"Too few for the Twelve Apostles." We both giggled.

Then Patty had an idea. "My seven-year-old boy is crazy about the Pokémon show on TV." She added, "We know the names of over two hundred of the characters."

"That ought to work."

We had struck the mother lode of naming possibilities. Patty began eagerly filling in blanks on the computer record form: Bulbasaur, Jigglypuff, Starmie, Pikachu . . .

I had formerly been a high school teacher, dealing with young people every day, but since my retirement I was out of the mainstream on such topics as Pokémon. I only recognized Pikachu, whose name I had heard on a trip to Japan two years before. I knew he was the best known of the Pokémon characters. Little did I guess how well known his namesake puppy would eventually become on Whidbey Island.

All eight of these Pokémon puppies looked alike. They were typical pound puppies: black, shorthaired, mixed-breeds with tuxedos—varied size white patches on their chests. All except one had a couple of white toes, in different places on different feet. This was the chief way we could tell them apart. Patty confined the four males together in one kennel and the four females in another. Neutered and spayed within a few days of their arrival, they bounced back immediately from their surgeries and became available for adoption.

For the first few weeks, other volunteers and I used to take all eight puppies to the exercise yards to let them romp and play together. Half the litter—two males and two females—were big and dominant, the "notice ME" bosses of the litter. These four were adopted in short order. That left Bulbasaur and Pikachu, the two smaller and shyer males, and Jigglypuff and Starmie, the remaining females and runts of the litter.

The latter four were very different from their dominant siblings: they were afraid of men, women, and children; they inhaled their food for fear of not getting enough; they were already used to being snarled at and picked on by their peers. Bulbasaur and Pikachu still tried to assert themselves in the group, without great success. Jigglypuff and Starmie soon gave up even trying.

All four of them were going to need a lot of work to become self-confident and more comfortable around people—in short, to become adoptable.

I often sat on a bench in the exercise yard to pet and play with the two shy females. The rest of the gang excluded them while they were off wrestling, chasing, barking, tumbling, and mounting one another to assert dominance. Sweet, unaggressive little souls, Jigglypuff and Starmie made perfect victims. I remember the whites of their eyes, how soft their fur felt, how much they belonged to each other and not to the rest of the litter.

Of all the volunteers, I was the one who ended up working with Jigglypuff and Starmie. This happened for several reasons. Before I began volunteering at WAIF, I had helped to found and run a wildlife rehabilitation clinic. There it had been among my tasks to find injured or abandoned wild animals, to bring them in, to help restore them to health, and, ultimately, to release them back into the wild. These animals ranged from rabbits and robins to seals, coyotes, deer, and eagles. To a greater or lesser extent, all of these animals shared a fear of humans, but they also had a strong will to live and a willingness to be helped—even by humans. I knew what it was to work with shy animals.

I was also fully retired, so I was able and willing to come to the shelter almost daily. And I had already experienced the deep rewards of helping two exceptionally insecure shelter dogs become more self-confident and seeing them better able to cope in life.

It was, in fact, because of a chance meeting with another special-needs dog ten years before that I had switched from the wildlife clinic, where I had been volunteering, to go to work for WAIF.

That, too, is a story worth telling.

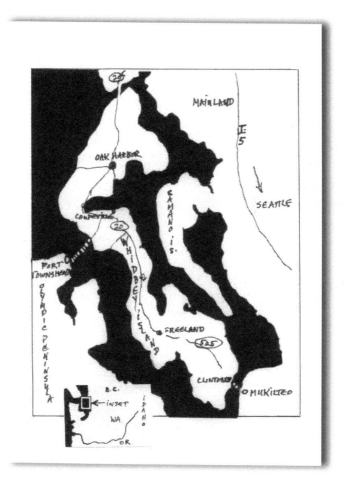

11.

Sweetie Gonzalez

October 1989

Working in my garden late on the last Saturday afternoon of October 1989, I looked up to see a strange-looking dog trotting north on West Beach Road. Dark gray and as big as a large German Shepherd, she held her head low and had about her an air of exhaustion. It was obvious she had just weaned puppies because her teats were still hanging down. Those teats looked like black leather; the dog had nursed many litters.

I called out to her but failed to get her attention. I watched her as she trotted on. That dog needed help. I could just feel it.

About an hour later my handsome Golden Retriever, Nacho, bounded into my car, and we set off for our end-of-the-afternoon walk on a beach not far from our house.

On the way home I saw the gray bitch foraging in the driftwood. There was an easy place to park, so I pulled over and got out of the car. She didn't run away. Instead, she raised her head to look at me.

"What do you think of the idea of coming home with us?" I asked, as I opened the rear car door.

She sized me up, then Nacho, and jumped into the car.

Looking at them in the rearview mirror I was surprised to see Nacho, a large male, quivering in fear of the bitch. No wonder!

She was bigger and older than he was, and I soon saw her utterly dominate him by holding the back of his neck in her jaws—mother-speak to a young dog. The translation: obey me!

When we got home, Nacho was relieved to get away from this new dog and to be let inside the house. The county animal shelter was already closed for the day so I prepared a bed for the gray dog in our garage. I wasn't about to let her into our house. Stray dogs and cats are always possible sources of diseases that can be contagious to resident pets. The strays need veterinary clearance before they can be safely introduced to a home environment. Besides, by the way this bitch had acted toward Nacho, I could well imagine she might love to eat our cats!

I stacked old newspapers about six inches high to build a bed up off the drafty floor and covered the bed with some draperies we no longer used. As I retrieved a water bowl on top of the freezer for the dog's use, I inadvertently knocked down a package of hamburger buns I'd bought earlier that afternoon. The dog beat me to them, and by the time I got there, she'd nudged the package to start working her way through the plastic wrapping. For a split second I hesitated to take them away from her. I didn't want her to bite me. Then I realized that I had better assert my dominance over her now, or else she would take control of me like she had Nacho.

I took the package from her—she allowed me to—but it was clear she was hungry and this was something she would like to eat. So, I opened the package and gave her one . . . and another . . . and another. She kept wolfing them down. Not a healthy diet, but the buns were just an appetizer. I would give her a nutritious dog dinner in a little while.

Feeding the buns to this dog gave me the opportunity to touch her. She reveled in the affectionate touching and leaned against me. As I stroked her, my fingers found about a half-inch of her choke chain collar ingrown in the skin of her neck. Both of her ears were abnormally thick and very sensitive to touch. She was thin but not emaciated. I took that to mean that she had not been on the road more than a few days. Her coat was dull, but her attitude seemed bright and she was very grateful to be gently handled. She recognized the bedding as her own, drank deeply of the water and relished the dry dog chow mixed with a small amount of hot water and canned dog food that I soon made for her.

She was a bright dog—a quick study—so I named her Speedy Gonzalez and planned to take her to the vet the next day to get her the basic vaccinations, have the ingrown chain removed and her ears examined.

The next day, Sunday, Speedy and I went to a veterinarian who had weekend office hours. The dog trusted me to hold her as the vet cut the embedded links with wire cutters, removed the collar, and treated the wound. He examined her ears, thick as the side of a man's hand and misshapen, like an ex-prize-fighter's cauliflower ears. He said the dog had a severe and long-term ear infection. He could perform surgery, but because the infection was so deep and close to the brain, the outcome would certainly be a total loss of hearing. That is, if she lived. The cost for surgery would be $500 to $1,000.

I wasn't happy with this diagnosis. Speedy wasn't my dog. I wasn't sure I wanted to subject her to a surgery she might not even survive, not to mention committing as much as $1,000 to an operation with such negative prospects. I needed more time and, possibly, a second opinion.

We returned home, and the dog once again bedded down comfortably in the garage.

That same night my friend Pam Lock phoned to ask me to reconsider an invitation I had earlier declined: to join the board of directors of a new organization she was forming. This was WAIF, the acronym for Whidbey Animals' Improvement Foundation. Earlier that summer, Pam had led a small group of young women to begin a community fund-raising effort, Cover the Critters, to provide a partial roof over the dogs at the Oak Harbor city dog pound. Their success in this initial endeavor spurred Pam to consider the formation of WAIF. I think Pam wanted me onboard because of my hands-on experience, not just with animals, but also with jumping through state government hoops to form a non-profit organization.

Five years before I had helped to form another animal rescue organization, this one dealing not with domestic animals but with wildlife. This had been a satisfying and totally involving experience for me, but I'd had some hints that it might be time for me to make a change.

For one thing, my husband, Curt, was beginning to express his uneasiness that I frequently had to go out alone to answer a call about an injured animal. I sometimes had the help of an excellent partner who lived not far from me, but he wasn't always available. More often than not, I had to drop whatever I was doing, pack up my rescue kit, and go alone to try to find the injured animal.

Whidbey Island is located in the northwest corner of Washington state. It is only eight miles wide at its widest point, but it is sixty miles long from north to south, and the drive alone might take forty to fifty minutes and often lead me into an unfamiliar area. Global positioning satellites and cell phones did not exist in 1989—or, if they did, I didn't have access to these technologies—so before I left home, I would try to call someone I knew in the rescue area to help me. Frequently, there was no one I knew or could reach in the area.

En route I would think about how I was going to approach the animal, what I needed to do and what kind of help I might need from other sources. The animals ranged from larger ones, such as seals, deer, or large birds—eagles, hawks, seagulls, herons, or swans—to smaller ones like raccoons, rabbits, squirrels, and smaller birds such as songbirds.

While driving, in addition to planning I also prayed, fervently, that I would find the help that I needed, whatever it might be. I always received it — often from complete strangers.

My long-suffering husband, who so graciously indulged me and let me pursue my own interests, also worried about the uncertainty and possible danger inherent in these jaunts. Sometimes I was gone for hours, searching without success. Sometimes I found the animal dead. Always, the creatures that I did find alive acted grateful for my help, despite the fact that they would have fled from me had they been able. But there was still the nagging prospect of the one that would get loose in the back of my car while I was bringing it to the veterinarian for help.

I restrained the deer I brought in by tying them to a weathered plywood board that I found on the beach with long cloth strips cut from bathrobe belts, mattress covers, or blankets found at garage sales. The board fit inside the back of my car when the rear seats were folded down. The deer always seemed comfortable when the car was accelerating, but they became nervous and agitated whenever the car was slowing down. If I had to stop to restrain the animal again, it was very possible the deer could damage itself, me, the car, or any combination of the three.

And added to any physical danger was potential legal jeopardy. The state of Washington was beginning to regulate the treatment of wild animals more stringently. The veterinarian who worked with our group had all the necessary licenses at the state and federal levels, but our volunteers now needed to have specific wildlife rescue training as well, and the state was putting in more strict controls for holding facilities. It felt like trying to help while being put into handcuffs, and the experience became more and more frustrating.

Wildlife rescue and rehabilitation was a new effort in the late '80s. I had taken and passed all the necessary instruction required by the state, but still there wasn't much information to go on. There was little printed material on the subject around at that time, and online information was still a thing of the future. I found the work challenging and exciting—one of the most interesting things I've ever done. We solved a lot of the problems we encountered with ingenuity and common sense.

Yet I also knew that my husband, at least, would be relieved if I stepped away from the potentially hazardous wild animals.

So, while I was talking with Pam, I told her about my encounter with Speedy Gonzalez, and also about the diagnosis that surgery was the only option.

"You do need a second opinion," Pam said. "I'll go with you tomorrow to see Donald Caldwell. He helps us with the shelter dogs."

We met at Dr. Caldwell's office the next day. Speedy was so easy to manage and so friendly to Pam and to the vet, that I decided her name wasn't Speedy at all. She became Sweetie Gonzalez.

This veterinarian concurred that Sweetie had a serious, long-term ear infection, but his prescribed protocol was more to my liking. "We'll start her out with ear drops," he said. "These must be given regularly: four times each day, without fail. We'll do this for a few weeks and see what develops."

"And surgery?"

"Certainly not at this point. We'll try this first and see what develops."

This diagnosis satisfied me and gave me the impetus to switch my volunteer efforts to WAIF. By now the wildlife clinic was well established and could do without me. My move would please my husband because it would take a while for him to find out that working with domestic animals can sometimes be as challenging as wild ones.

The fit with WAIF felt right.

In just these two days Sweetie and I had become attached to one another—*bonded* is the word often used for this wonderful process. I wanted to give this dog the necessary daily care myself, not surrender her to the shelter, not risk having her former owner reclaim her, not risk having her put down because, in shelter parlance, she "ran out of time." If a shelter animal was not adopted within the prescribed time limit, the animal was put to death. I speak more about that in the next chapter.

So, back Sweetie and I went to our garage, where I continued to carefully quarantine her from our other pets. But I needed to do something to help Sweetie pass the time besides just resting, eating, and having drops massaged into her ears four times a day. I decided to give her obedience training when I walked her—which I continued to do separately from Nacho.

I believe that giving dogs an education in what people expect of them is as crucial as giving an education to human children. Besides teaching dogs useful behavior boundaries, giving them an understanding of how to please people is fundamental to their survival. It is especially important for large dogs, since many people regard a dog's size alone as a threat, regardless of the animal's personality. Besides, I knew that training Sweetie would help me control her if I had to take her inside my house during the increasingly cold weather. She was still very much an alpha female, but she needed to recognize me as her leader and I had to enforce her cooperation at all times.

Sweetie was a dream to teach: so quick to learn, so anxious to please, so proud of herself when she won my approval. And she was such a good laugher! She fairly chuckled out loud when we played hide and seek, fetch, and "gonna getcha"—where I chased after her, growling and laughing, arms open wide and threatening to grab her while she dodged delightedly to avoid capture. By the end of November, she had gained confidence as well as weight. Lights glowed in her formerly dull coat. Her ears seemed to be less painful and sensitive. She clearly reveled in the attention she was getting.

There was just one problem: I was to have long-scheduled surgery on both my feet in early December. I wouldn't be able to do my usual walking for several weeks.

We decided to move Sweetie out of our increasingly wintry garage and into Dr. Caldwell's facility to board. There she would receive her daily eardrops and the care she needed.

I phoned often to check on Sweetie. Usually I got positive reports, but the day I talked to the kennel-cleaning woman, she said, "That's the dumbest dog I've ever seen in my life!"

I was shocked both by her words and by her emphatic tone of voice.

"Doesn't act like any other dog I've ever seen," the woman said. "She's so stupid. She's so stubborn."

I listened to the cleaning woman drone on, pouring out her complaints. I didn't ask for details. Clearly, Sweetie was sweet and smart with people who respected her and uncooperative with those who didn't. Even if I had tried to tell this woman about my experience with Sweetie, I knew she would never have believed my account of the dog's quickness and willingness to please.

I had to get Sweetie out of there, but I still wasn't able to take care of her at home. Dr. Caldwell, Pam, and I decided that she should go to the county-run Whidbey Island Animal Shelter. With Sweetie living in the county shelter, I couldn't wait to get back on my feet to start helping WAIF and the shelter give the best care it could to her—and to all the other animals there.

Sweetie Gonzalez

III.

More on Sweetie Gonzalez

1989 - 1990

When Sweetie Gonzalez went to the Whidbey Island Animal Shelter in December 1989, she had a much better chance to continue living than she might have had just a few short months earlier. Whidbey Animals' Improvement Foundation (WAIF) had become legally incorporated as a non-profit organization at the end of 1989, and the manager of the shelter welcomed its minimal-kill premise.

During the 1980s, as an offshoot of the women's rights movement, a worldwide revolution that came to be known as the animal rights movement began to change the public attitude toward animals, both wild and domestic. On Whidbey Island, WAIF was part of this movement. Had WAIF not been successful, the story of both Sweetie and, later, Pikachu would have ended in death not long after the animals' surrender.

One of the WAIF founders was an airline flight attendant whose husband had international connections in the animal-care world. This is how the idea of a minimal-kill animal shelter came earlier to our corner of the world than it did to many other places. WAIF was one of the first organizations in the Pacific Northwest to make the leap from an old-fashioned dog pound—a holding place—to a true animal shelter, which is a haven.

The dog pound theory had long been in use: lost, stray, abandoned, surrendered, or impounded pets were confined in an area designated by local government as a holding area. If these unwanted dogs and cats were not reclaimed or adopted within a certain time limit, usually five days, the community-contracted pound manager or animal control officer killed them or took them to a veterinarian to be humanely killed in order to make space for the next equally unfortunate dogs and cats to appear. Euphemisms such as *euthanizing, putting to sleep,* or *putting down* softened the shocking starkness of this official and legally sanctioned act of killing animals.

The reasoning was that it cost money to feed and clean up after unwanted animals. Why spend much taxpayer money on them? Why, for instance, provide them with a pleasant place to be? The location of the public pound served as a good indicator of the respect humans had for animals: Island County's dog pound was located at the county dump in Central Whidbey. The thinking was that the dump was the most convenient place for these dogs, since most of the carcasses would end up there anyhow.

Once in a while a pound manager gambled and kept an exceptionally desirable dog longer than the time limit—meaning that its care cost more than the budgeted allowance—because he could charge more for its adoption and perhaps make a little money on the side.

Shelter managers rarely had any qualms about dispatching cats and dogs suffering from upper respiratory disease, otherwise known as the common cold, because the disease was contagious and no one had considered taking precautions to prevent the disease or giving the animals medical treatment. That cost money.

Not only could a pet be killed for having a cold, it could be put to death for even more trivial reasons.

Not long after my husband and I brought home the young purebred Golden Retriever, an abandoned dog, who became our beloved Nacho, the county animal control officer phoned me to say she'd taken in another young Golden Retriever with severely matted and tangled hair. "Would you like another one?" she asked me.

I told her that one new pet was all I could handle at the moment.

A few days later when I went to the pound, I asked to see the Golden Retriever.

"Oh, it was put down."

I got goose bumps. I had never dreamed that the dog would be killed because the animal needed a haircut.

No wonder it was common for island residents to abandon their unwanted pets to the wild rather than to almost certain death at the pound!

Often, the callousness with which people surrendered their pets was just as outrageous as the reasons for euthanasia. The most shocking case that I remember was of the couple that had remodeled their home and changed its color scheme. Since their pets no longer "went with" the new colors, they surrendered them.

WAIF's minimal-kill animal shelter alternative concept would cost more in all ways: space, food, time, labor. *Minimal kill* meant animals would be put to death only if they were known biters, terminally ill or injured or proven to be aggressive. *Minimal kill* also meant potential pets would be maintained in the shelter however long it took to find them suitable homes.

But could this humane theory become practice? Could the pound be transformed into a true shelter, a haven for animals, a place where many of them would live in better conditions than in their previous homes? Could these animals be kept healthy, physically and mentally, for the indefinite length of time it might take to find them a good home? And could an animal support organization raise the money needed to provide a safe and clean shelter, as well as food and medical attention? Would that organization be able to attract the needed volunteer labor for cleaning, exercising, and hands-on care? And what about advertising to make the public aware of healthy pets available for adoption?

Earlier in 1989, Pam Lock had organized the Cover the Critters campaign that I mentioned before. Leadership of Cover the Critters was made up of Oak Harbor business and professional women and wives of active duty U.S. Navy personnel stationed at nearby Whidbey Island Naval Air Station.

These volunteers had found that the city pound, located in a small obscure spot on the old Navy seaplane base property, consisted solely of a chain-link fenced yard. The dogs were protected from the elements by only a couple of portable, heavy-duty white plastic igloo-shaped doghouses with built-in raised floors. There were not nearly enough of them for all the dogs to stay inside a structure.

The dog yard was wide open to almost constant wind—plus rain, sleet, snow, and sun—and the ground, with just a few patches of grass, was either mud or dust. The dogs lived as a pack, each one dominating or being dominated by other dogs. The boss-dogs got the lion's share of the food; others got little or nothing.

The dogs were the responsibility of a city-employed animal control officer, whose job was mainly to enforce animal ordinances. The pound existed as a place to reclaim lost or impounded dogs. Few attempts were made to place unclaimed dogs for adoption because such efforts cost money. No support organization existed; none was encouraged. The city animal control officer did not welcome what he considered interference in doing his job, although he did agree to accept the new roof.

In fact, the community fund-raising effort to put a roof over the Oak Harbor city dog yard was such a success that the Cover the Critters group, now morphing to become WAIF, decided to tackle the task of upgrading the county pound, the Whidbey Island Animal Shelter (WIAS) in Coupeville.

At the time, the WIAS manager was a tireless and caring young Navy wife named Shelley, who knew it would take a lot of support to make WIAS live up to its name as an animal shelter. She was more than willing to accept the help of WAIF, Pam, and her volunteers in doing that.

WAIF volunteers went to work, just as they had done with Oak Harbor's city pound—buying and donating materials and labor to build a roof extending from the existing building partway over the outdoor animal pens.

The antiquated WIAS building, which contained an office shared by the shelter manager and the animal control officer, had some temperature controls, but the few indoor kennels, like the outdoor pens, offered little relief from either heat or cold. Since one indoor kennel always had to be left empty for an emergency, there was little available housing space indoors.

Most of the dogs were kept outside in large pens with dirt floors, enclosed with chain link fences. Each outdoor pen usually housed an average of six to twelve dogs. All the dogs shared two or three igloo doghouses per pen.

The dogs also shared one large, galvanized iron bucket of water per pen. In winter, the water turned to solid ice. The water was only slightly less likely to freeze in the indoor kennels.

When the summer sun beat down, there was no shade—no escaping the sun until the long shadows of late afternoon and early evening.

When it rained, everything turned to mud. Feces and urine mixed with mud made the pens impossible to clean. The dogs were always filthy.

Because Island County ordinances addressed only the care of dogs, Whidbey Island was rife with feral cats. Having no local place to surrender cats when necessary, residents —frequently, though not always, military personnel being rotated—often abandoned them. These healthy adult female pet cats were capable of having several litters of kittens a year and unless the kittens were literally handled—that is, physically touched—by people, they grew up as wild animals. The term *feral* refers to animals of any domestic species that have grown up as wild animals or have reverted to being wild, with little or no hands-on socialization by humans.

One of the first changes that Shelley and WAIF made at the Coupeville shelter was to provide care for cats as well as dogs. WAIF volunteers pitched in to remodel part of the existing building to make space for some cat cages. An anonymous donor made a generous gift of twelve brand new stainless steel cages. This was exciting for two reasons: WAIF volunteers now had the necessary cleanable housing to care for cats and, just as important, it was an impressive show of support for WAIF from the community.

But there was so much more to be done. The tap water at the dump smelled putrid and had been officially declared undrinkable. Safe water had to be purchased and provided for humans. Staff and volunteers hauled water from their homes in plastic jugs for the cats. The dogs had to make do with smelly water.

As conditions at the dump gradually became publically recognized, an ecologically correct overhaul was planned and, in time, executed. Some of the areas where we used to walk dogs were declared off-limits for the safety of both the volunteers and the dogs. A vast field of formerly loose trash blowing in the wind was covered over. Methane gas was piped to an apparatus that burned it off, creating a kind of eternal flame not far from the shelter building.

As soon as I could walk following my foot surgery, I started showing up at the shelter to volunteer. From early 1990 until late 1995, in addition to being a member of the WAIF's board of directors, I cleaned cat cages, scooped poop, walked and watered dogs, collected and laundered animal bedding. I trapped feral cats and socialized them in my home so they could become available for adoption. I photographed animals and submitted Pet of the Week copy to the three island weekly newspapers, the monthly *Whidbey Magazine,* and the bi-monthly *Mutt Matchers Messenger,* which was distributed to all of western Washington. I wrote the WAIF quarterly newsletter—our single largest fundraiser—as well as maintaining the mailing list and the annual record of financial contributions. I created roadside signs asking military motorists to include WAIF in their Combined Federal Campaign dona-tions, formulated informational brochures, spoke to charitable groups requesting grants, placed weekly classified "found" ads, as well as display ads in island publications.

What had started for me as a few hours a week walking dogs morphed during five years into averaging over forty hours a week of volunteer work for WAIF.

It was a period of great change for WAIF. A serious personal health crisis forced Pam Lock to direct her energies away from volunteer work and into surviving. The flight attendant who had been so influential in advocating minimal-kill lost a policy battle on the board and quit the organization. She had advocated depicting piteous WAIF animals behind bars, and when the board of directors chose, instead, to feature success stories and happy endings, she left. New leaders joined the group.

By the time I resigned from the WAIF board of directors in 1995 to resume the hobbies, pastimes, friends, classes, organizations, and social engagements I had given up over the years when WAIF was my top priority, it had gone from being a hopeful experiment to becoming a thriving organization, an island institution, respected and appreciated in the community and copied elsewhere in Washington State. A second building had been constructed and the original one remodeled. With much trepidation, the board of directors had successfully risked hiring a paid executive director. WAIF was looking down the road to try to obtain the City of Oak Harbor and Island County contracts to run those respective shelters and, eventually, to build a shelter of its own.

As for my Sweetie Gonzalez, because of her fierce dominance, she was separated from other dogs and housed in one of the indoor kennels. That special creature would begin howling in her kennel when she recognized the sound of my car on the road approaching the shelter. And when I left the premises, I heard her howling until the car was out of earshot. I always walked her and spent time with her on my frequent visits. I featured her among the WAIF dogs in the March – April 1990 *Mutt Matchers Messenger*, and her photo caught the eye of a young woman in the Olympia, Washington, area who worked with state prison inmates.

"She has just the same look in her eyes as the prisoners," Ellen remarked, when she had traveled the long distance from Olympia to the shelter to adopt Sweetie.

We talked on the phone over the next few months to share progress reports. At first it was good news, but gradually more and more time went by without contact. One day I phoned and found Ellen very upset: her difficult divorce had just become final; Sweetie had attacked her cat, and when she spoke harshly to Sweetie, Sweetie had tried to bite the backs of her ankles. She wasn't sure what would come of all this.

I didn't dare to call again.

I had always wondered about Sweetie's wolf-iness, but when I heard she had gone for the backs of Ellen's legs—clearly a wolf trait—I was finally certain. Sweetie had been a hybrid-wolf puppy factory: a half-wolf bitch bred continuously for the profit of her original owner, who sold Sweetie's one-quarter wolf puppies.

It had taken the gift of a half-wild dog for me to transition from rescuing wildlife to rescuing domestic dogs.

IV.

Early Work

When I left the WAIF board in 1995, I took art classes in painting and design and went back to playing golf. But I did miss the animals. I had a persistent feeling that there were special needs animals I should devote time to. I wanted no further part of the infighting and politics inherent in leadership, but after a few months I offered my services to WAIF to simply walk dogs. That's why I happened to be present at the shelter that April day in 2000 when the Pokémon puppies entered our lives and also why I wound up devoting time to them—first to Jigglypuff and Starmie, later to Pikachu.

To get an idea how different Jigglypuff and Starmie were from most shelter dogs, I must describe the walking procedure for a typical shelter dog.

The small, easy-to-handle dogs rarely needed to be walked at the shelter. When they did come in, they were often invited to spend time in the office, where they were more visible to the public than in the kennels. Although they stayed for the prescribed time—giving their owners a chance to reclaim them—these small dogs always seemed to be adopted within minutes of their arrival.

So the dog-walking volunteers were left with medium-sized to large dogs—the 35- to 100-plus-pound bundles of boundless energy, many of them surrendered precisely because their owners had found them too unruly to handle.

Pee, poop, blood, sweat, ear-splitting noise, and occasional tears: that, in a nutshell, was the story of walking a typical shelter dog.

Before I selected a dog for walking, I would pocket a few treats and choose a choke chain or harness and a sturdy leash the right size and strength for the dog to be walked. I also coiled my own twenty-foot-long leash around my neck for ready access once we got outside.

All the dogs whose kennels were on the same side of the shelter as the dog to be walked reacted wildly when they spotted a volunteer preparing to choose one. All the dogs wanted to be The One. Most would stand on their hind legs at the door to their kennel, barking, squirming, eager to go. Some may once have been trained, but after a few days at the shelter, they reverted to extreme behavior, jumping, twisting, bouncing against the walls, running back and forth in their kennels: anything to get attention; anything to get out.

The cement floors of the kennels were usually wet from hosing that was done to clean them. That made the footing slick, both for the dogs and for me.

Once I'd chosen a dog to walk, I had to plan how to open the door to his kennel as little as possible and yet squeeze inside, all the while blocking the dog's escape. I also had to avoid stepping in slippery urine puddles or piles of feces, or worse yet, getting knocked down in them by a jumping dog. Now, at least, each kennel usually held only one dog.

At that time none of the dogs wore collars inside their kennels. Even if a dog had been admitted wearing a collar, it was hung high on the door and, hopefully, someone remembered to put it on them when they were adopted. Being collarless prevented the collar from accidentally getting caught and hung up on the link metal fencing, but, in my opinion, if the dogs had been wearing collars, it would have been a whole lot easier to catch them for walks because most dogs were so excited and eager to get out that they resisted having a collar put on.

Like other volunteers, I soon adopted several strategies. Once inside the kennel, instead of moving around and chasing the dog, I would stand tall in one place, rotating so my back was always to the dog until it calmed down. The dog, in turn, would be trying to face me, to stand on its hind legs, and to jump on my front side. A mother dog disciplines her unruly pups by showing them her behind, so turning my backside to them was behavior they understood. Usually, it worked.

Next, I threaded the hook end of a leash back through its handle to make a big slipknot, which I quickly looped around the dog's neck to get temporary control. Then I was able to slip a chain collar over the dog's head.

Once the collar was in place, I removed the slipknot, hooked the leash to the choke chain, and we were ready to set off. Like a rodeo bull-rider, I adjusted my last handhold, swung open the door, and we were *out the chute.*

Outside the kennel door, we ran the gauntlet past the doors of other dogs' kennels, all of them rushing to see which dog was out, then barking at it furiously and jealously. This was often terrifying for the dog being walked, but it was an undeniable part of the pack experience and it seemed unavoidable. When this dog got back to his kennel, he would do the same thing to the next dog being walked.

Once past the deafening roar of all the frenzied, yapping dogs, we would have to stop at a second door in the outer perimeter chain link fence. I had to open it while the excited dog jumped and strained impatiently to GO, *NOW!*

Finally, the second door secured behind us, the now liberated dog would swiftly rush to the end of its leash, almost jerking my arms out of their sockets.

None of these dogs owed allegiance to his walker. If a dog was ever lucky enough to get five walks in a week's time, it was usually with five different walkers. So, the dog didn't begin to have the consideration that a longtime pet has for his owner.

Beyond the outer perimeter fence, a dirt road wound around the huge sunken pit of the dump, several football fields wide and long. Once on the road, I would attach my twenty-foot leash to the dog's chain collar, remove his short leash, and tie it around my waist. The dog was then free to go off the road into the surrounding grass to pee and poop, which he was eager to do outside the confines of his kennel because no animal likes to foul its own nest. After that we set off into the woods.

Ah, the delicious smells! I always stopped whenever the dog wanted to, and we walked for about a half hour before heading back toward the shelter. By that time, the dog was no longer in the itching-to-get-out stage, and I would work with him to heel, sit, and briefly stay. I knew if the dog had some manners, he would be more appealing to a potential adopter.

Then, we would find ourselves a pleasant place to sit and just spend some quiet time. By that stage, the dog would be acting like he belonged to me. That is, until we got back within hearing distance of the shelter.

There, the all-out, frenzied barking resumed as we approached, entered the outer door, and again walked past the kennels with the dogs charging, challenging, barking. The dog I was walking was tired by that time. He went willingly back into his kennel. I removed his collar and the long lead and made sure his water bowl was full. He was as glad to be back as he had been glad to leave.

I'd spray the collar, leash, and my hands with a bleach solution to try to prevent spreading any germs to the next dog they touched, and I'd plod through the footbath to disinfect my boots before I entered the next kennel.

While taking this breather, I'd wipe the sweat off my head, neck and face and check for bloody scratches, nicks, or cuts. When a dog jumps all over you, his long claws inevitably damage skin and clothing. Fortunately, there was never much blood, and it was always my own —not the dog's.

After a walk, each volunteer recorded in a notebook the name of the dog, their own name, the date and time of the walk, and any comments on the dog's behavior that could be useful to shelter personnel and other walkers. It was particularly helpful to know if a dog was aggressive or an extreme puller. The records helped me to choose not *if* but *when* I would walk a particular dog. I tried to walk the difficult ones first, when I had more energy; the easier, more compliant ones later, when I was tired.

In early May 2000, shelter staff separated the remaining four-month-old Pokémon puppies, each into their own kennel. I no longer had much contact with Pikachu and Bulbasaur because, although they were still rather unassertive and shy, they were managing quite well with shelter life, volunteers, staff members, and prospective adopters. Jigglypuff and Starmie, however, were another matter entirely. Soon I committed to working with them every day.

Even though the two dogs were now independent and no longer able to imitate and learn from each other, it was uncanny how they still behaved in almost identical ways. When I entered the clanking metal door, for instance, Jigglypuff and Starmie would each shrink and huddle against the rear wall of their kennel, fear gleaming in their eyes. Instead of brashly jumping on me in eagerness to go for a walk, they would each cower in a corner to avoid being collared and leashed. They wouldn't make direct eye contact and never wagged their tail. On the other hand, neither of them was ever aggressive. They wanted only to run and hide, never to threaten or bite. My options were to either drag these dogs outside or pick them up and carry them out past the furious tumult of barking dogs. And since they each weighed only about fifteen pounds, it was easiest and most compassionate for me to carry them out.

Once outside, when their feet touched the ground, Jigglypuff and Starmie would stand, tails between their hind legs reaching so far forward it almost touched their front legs, and wait. Totally submissive. No eager pulling. No joy in movement. No happy exploration of The Great Outside World. Just fear and anxiety.

I had never before encountered any dog that huddled behind me, that did not want to be out in front of me. I didn't know what to do with either one of them. And they didn't know what to do with me.

Helpless, I would squat down and gently stroke the dog, saying softly, "Hey, baby, it's me again. I'm here for you. Don't you want to go for a little walk?" I encouraged them to smell me, tried to get them to feel comfortable with me, tried to earn their trust—to no avail. I offered treats; they ignored them.

After a few minutes, I would turn away and set off, walking. When I felt a tug at the end of the leash, I'd looked back and usually found the dog still sitting there, now being tipped forward by the pull of the leash.

It was not good, and I didn't understand why it was happening. The behavior was peculiar to these two dogs. They were unlike any other dog I'd ever encountered, and they were unlike the rest of the dogs in their own litter. Even though I didn't walk Pikachu and Bulbasaur, I knew they didn't remain rooted to the ground!

So, I would walk back, pick up the dog—either Jigglypuff or Starmie—and carry her forward to the spot where I had stopped. Then I placed her again on the ground and resumed walking. After days of this, I just began to drag the dog, as mercifully as I could. She finally began to run along, but chose to trail behind me, never walking by my side, and, never, God forbid, walking out in front of me.

Even so, it was some progress.

In mid May there was a kennel cough outbreak at the shelter. Kennel cough is an upper respiratory disease that is contagious among dogs and difficult to control when dogs are living together. It's not usually life threatening, but the dogs feel sick and it's hard for the people around them to hear them hacking and rasping. In spite of all our precautions, the illness spread throughout the dogs at the shelter and our remaining Pokémon puppies got it as well.

The only apparent way to halt the contagion was a total lockdown so that as time passed the infected areas would become less virulent and the dogs themselves had a chance to recover. If volunteers were willing to change clothes and shoes and wash all exposed areas, including skin and hair, immediately afterward, they were permitted to work with a single dog per day inside its kennel. Otherwise, the dogs were totally off-limits to volunteers: no exercise yard, no walks, no handling. Only cleaning and feeding by shelter staff. This protocol lasted for two full consecutive weeks, and then had to be repeated during several successive outbreaks of the disease over the next few months.

Thus, at a stage in their lives crucial to their social development with people, the Pokémon puppies had virtually no human contact. Given their early experience as tiny pups in a less-than-loving and possibly abusive home, their strange genetic wiring, and their lack of socialization in the shelter, the pups had a mountain of obstacles to overcome in their later lives.

At last, in June, some good news: Bulbasaur was adopted. That meant there were three Pokémon puppies left.

Throughout the summer, whenever contact with volunteers was permitted, I continued to work with Jigglypuff and Starmie. They both finally caught on to the idea that taking a walk was a nice break from the kennel, but still they walked without enthusiasm or energy, trailing behind me.

Still, I did what I could to vary their experience of being out of the kennel in order to prepare these frightened dogs for life in the great big world. I walked them in the cool shade of the woods and on the hot, dusty road around the dump pit. Also, I'd lift them into my car and drive on the road inside the dump. Jigglypuff seemed to enjoy these rides but, without fail, Starmie got carsick.

Because I had some seniority among the volunteers, the shelter manager permitted me to take the dogs off site. As often as I could, I took either Jigglypuff or Starmie home with me for a few hours at a time. I wanted to give them some controlled exposure to new experiences in order to build their self-confidence.

I can't say this was an unqualified success. For one thing, they were both absolutely terrified of our cats. One time Jigglypuff and I were sitting on the bed in the guest room when Terrible

Tyrannosaurus Tessa, our fifteen-pound domestic long-haired grey and white cat, waddled into the doorway and boldly looked in Jigglypuff's direction. The dog tensed and quivered. The cat took two steps into the room, and the dog bolted in retreat, attempting to climb the wall to get away. I caught Jigglypuff by the collar, held her close to me, and tried to calm her. Tessa gave her a withering look and stomped away, sure she need not bother to do anything more to intimidate this wimp. And she was right.

I took the dogs to the beach, where their Labrador Retriever genes surged to the fore. They both loved wading in the water and played at fetching sticks, awkward as that was when they were at the end of a twenty-foot leash.

Most gratifying was one Sunday afternoon when I brought Jigglypuff along with me to work in our garden. For the first hour she sat up, watchful and alert, looking for any unexpected movement, listening for any unfamiliar sound. I stayed close by, kneeling to work in a particular patch with the dog's long lead looped around my ankle, and after some time she dug herself a little nest in the earth, under the shade of a fir tree, and fell sound asleep.

Perhaps the dog was exhausted, but I took it as a sign of trust.

PETS OF THE WEEK 6/23/00

Starmie

Jiggly Puff

Bob

Pikachu

Bulbasaur

Pepper-mint

V.

Starmie's First Escape

The first episode of what later became an escape theme with variations took place one Saturday afternoon in July when I was walking Starmie in a park at the beach not far from our house. We'd gone down a trail that paralleled the beach and were about a half-mile from where we'd started at the parking lot and picnic grounds. Starmie was close to me, so there was no tension to hold the collar tight. She slowed down and lowered her head. To the utter surprise of both of us, the choke chain relaxed and the enlarged loop fell off her neck and onto the ground with a clink. Stunned, I found myself holding a long leash and an empty collar. Starmie stood a few feet away, buck naked, looking as shocked as I was.

Then I made one of my many mistakes in dealing with the wary Pokémon clan. At least I knew enough not to chase her. Perhaps if I had immediately squatted down and urged her to come to me, she might have done so. But I remained standing, towering over the dog, and moved toward her, holding out the circle of the collar.

Not on your life! I'm sure her Border Collie genes kicked in. Border Collies are sharp-eyed and quick. Starmie began backing away from me. I could almost see the wheels turning in her head.

Then came the moment—I could see the shock of pleasure in her eyes—when the dog knew she was on her own. She was *free!* She was the one calling the shots.

For a moment neither of us knew what to do. I turned and walked slowly in the opposite direction, and Starmie followed me, just out of reach. I noticed some people approaching, and I knew the activity would spook her and she'd run away. I turned back the way I had come. She turned and again followed me. We went some distance, and the dog stayed fairly close to me, but because it was a summer weekend afternoon, there were a lot of people in the park. I wasn't going to be able to lead Starmie through these people all the way back to my car, and we couldn't wait for hours until everyone left.

Finally, and inevitably, Starmie dashed into a wooded area, leaving me behind.

My heart plummeted and along with it went my pride at being the only volunteer trusted to take dogs off the shelter premises. I hurried back to the picnic area, borrowed a cell phone, and called the shelter to make the dreaded report that I had lost Starmie. There weren't enough people available, volunteers or staff, to mount a search effort that afternoon. Feeling incompetent, I returned home. I knew there was no point in my trying to get Starmie back with weekend crowds around.

Yet I had to do something. Coyote packs, known to prey on domestic cats and dogs, populated the backwoods of the park. And there were bald eagles, as well. From my wildlife days I knew of an eagle that had picked up a fawn, and I had seen eagles carry off mature Canada geese. At thirty pounds, little Starmie might be too heavy for that fate—I prayed so—but I knew it would be a scary night for a nervous dog alone in the wild.

I phoned a friend who owned a humane trap of a suitable size for Starmie, told him my troubles, and asked to borrow it. He brought it right over. At dusk, when most people had left the park, I returned with the trap. Made of metal wire, it was a long, low, rectangular box with a door at only one end. At the opposite, closed end was a small metal platform set on top of a spring-loaded mechanism. Just beyond that, wedged against the far end, I set a small bowl of dry dog chow—Starmie's normal meal at the shelter. I was tempted to make it more attractive by adding some canned dog food, but decided against that because I didn't want to make the trap too attractive to other animals. Any creature entering the trap would spring the door by putting its weight on the platform to get at the food. The door would quickly snap shut behind it.

Choosing to place the trap at an intersection of main trails in the woods, not far from a picnic table, I put a large bowl of fresh water next to it. Even if Starmie didn't enter the trap, I wanted her to be able to drink freely. She would be stressed enough physically and psychologically without the additional problem of dehydration.

I didn't want to spend the night in the park myself: it just wasn't safe. Over the many years I had walked there, I had seen teens set off fireworks in the bathroom and addicts using drugs in the parking lot. I knew that the ranger had driven off a group of guys who had made themselves a hidden bedroom in the woods, but I wasn't sure the fix was permanent. So, I returned home, determined to check the trap every two hours throughout the night or until I caught her. I prayed aloud that it would be Starmie I would catch—not a coyote, otter, or raccoon.

At 10:00 I lay down, fully dressed, on the living room couch, setting the alarm clock on the coffee table next to me. When it rang at midnight, I was quite alert and sprang up eagerly to drive the five minutes to the park and check the trap.

I parked the car outside the closed gate and tiptoed quietly into the dark woods to the trap.

Empty. The food untouched.

Driving back home I saw a group of teen-aged kids on the side of the road. I stepped on the gas, glad not to have to deal with them.

Back to the couch.

At 2:00 a.m. the shrill alarm awakened me again. This time I was a little slower to get going. A pale, last-quarter moon was rising in the northeastern sky. I found the trap empty.

At 4:00 a.m., struggling to awaken in the gray light of early dawn, I dragged myself off the couch, plodded to the garage, drove to the park, and checked the trap. Empty. Thank God that no one else was in it, but maybe it was just too scary for any critter. It was important to let Starmie know that she was not totally abandoned, that someone was still looking out for her, caring for her. I decided to remove the bowl of dry dog food and set it on the ground outside the trap—for whatever animal wanted to eat it.

At 6:00 a.m. it was daylight, and the trap still empty. A few bits of dry dog chow were scattered on the ground around the mostly empty bowl. The level of water was lower than before. The question was: who had eaten and drunk? Starmie? Or another animal?

I was exhausted. Hoping that Starmie had gotten the nourishment and identified its source with a specific location in the park, I went home. Now that the dangers of night were past, I was only interested in taking care of myself and getting some sleep. I knew, however, that I would probably sleep for hours, so before I went to bed, I phoned the shelter and left a message on the answering machine. I reported what I had done throughout the night, the exact location of my friend's trap, and asked that, if possible, someone go to the park and pick the trap up so that it wasn't stolen when the first visitors of the day arrived. As for me, I hardly cared what happened right now: I had to go to bed.

In the early afternoon the sound of a ringing telephone awakened me. I jumped up to answer it and heard a joyous voice on the other end, "We caught Starmie!"

Grateful in a way that words cannot express, I said, "How on earth did you get her?"

"Darcy got her." Darcy was an off-duty staff member who had volunteered, along with a gang of others, mobilized after I phoned the previous day. They went to the park early that morning. On the basis of my message, they picked up the trap and then scattered into the woods. Darcy sat at the picnic table near where the trap had been located. As I had thought she might, Starmie appeared at that important intersection.

The dog and Darcy made eye contact. The dog started to sprint past. Darcy stuck out her arm, snagged Starmie, and hung on.

VI.

Piki's First Escape

July – September 2000

Sometime in mid July a young man came to the shelter looking for a second dog to adopt. He gave verbal commands in a firm voice to his young, black dog, Spike, who trailed him closely. Spike was off lead, which was unusual and impressive for *any* dog at the animal shelter. He was well behaved and self-confident, curiously un-rattled by the tumultuous barking. Spike seemed to know his way around the shelter. He looked familiar, so much like Pikachu....

My hopes soared, and I asked the man if he would look at Piki.

"No, I'm not interested in adopting Spike's brother."

Shocked, I asked if he remembered what Spike's shelter name had been.

"Bulbasaur."

So this young man had worked a miracle! Initially, I was crushed that he was unwilling to do the same for Piki. Then I saw that here, before me, was living proof that a miracle could be done. To see Bulbasaur —Spike—excel in this way made me sure that the other Pokémon puppies could do the same. They too could become normal dogs.

August 4, 2000, was a day that I didn't go to the shelter. It was the day that Pikachu was adopted.

Volunteers and employees are always elated when a shelter animal gets a good home, especially one who has been confined for a long time. But this time when we stopped in the office to cheer for Piki's adoption, the young woman on duty voiced some misgivings. She said the folks who took him hadn't paid much attention when she told them Piki was shy and fearful —far more so than a typical dog would be. She had cautioned them to keep him on a leash even *inside* the house until they were sure he had bonded with them and was at ease in his new home. She didn't feel quite sure they were the right people for Piki, but then again, she didn't want to prevent any shelter dog from going to a new and hopefully happy life.

About a week later, construction workers building a new home in the Bon Air region of Central Whidbey phoned the shelter to report an unsupervised, bone-thin, black dog raiding their trash cans daily. This was the same area as Pikachu's new home. A shelter employee phoned the new owners to see how he was doing.

"Well, we tied him outside in the back yard the day after he came home. Something spooked him. We couldn't figure out what."

So, on August 5 — perhaps twenty-four hours after his adoption and departure from the shelter — Pikachu had been frightened enough to break his rope and jump a fence. His new "family" hadn't cared enough to go looking for him or even to let the shelter know he was missing, so we could look for him.

Dogs and cats seldom stray far from where they have wandered away, been misplaced, lost, or dumped. Although books and movies about pets that have returned home after months or years of a cross-country journey are dramatic and well known, it is true of only a tiny minority of animals. Most will stay put within a small, neighboring area. Without anyone realizing it, Piki had simply moved next door from his adoptive home onto a large expanse of forested land owned by one of the Seattle-area software barons, whose vacation cabin was under construction.

Just as they had done when Starmie went missing, volunteers and off-duty staff members gathered at the construction site at every possible opportunity and fanned out into the brush. Despite the fact that all the Pokémon puppies had proven at the shelter that they could leap a five-foot high fence from a standing start and run like greyhounds, some young Navy men, recruited from the nearby base as volunteers, were quite certain they could run Piki down. They eventually spotted him and chased after him through the brush in mad pursuit. Entirely the wrong thing to do with a loose dog — ever! The chase wore out these fit young men and challenged their macho presumptions; all it did for Piki, I suspect, was to increase his terror of young men.

In fact, at that point Piki grew even more wary of people.

Because everyone had helped me recapture Starmie, it was only right that I help find Piki. I drove the twenty miles to Bon Air almost every day and searched the forest trails for evidence of our stray dog. I found marks of a dragged rope in the late summer dust and half-eaten cones fallen from fir trees. Occasionally I found dog tracks, but it was impossible to tell which dog had made them.

One day I crossed the highway that runs north to south up the entire length of Whidbey Island from the west side over to the east side. There, I found a spacious, fenced yard with a doghouse and many dog toys strewn around. I went to the door and asked the woman who answered my knock if she had seen a stray black dog in the neighborhood.

"That black devil dog!" she said, her voice rising and her face flushing with anger. "My bulldog is tied on a chain. That black dog jumps the fence *into* our yard to play with our dog, gets him all excited, and he chokes on his chain. Then that black dog grabs his toys and plays with them, right in front of him, just out of reach. Throws them all over the yard! I could kill him! Look what he did to my vacuum cleaner . . ."

Her metal vacuum cleaner attachment had been bent into a shape beyond reclamation. It looked like the work of my Pikachu. I figured he would be at the teething stage just about now.

I thanked her and handed her a twenty-dollar bill, saying, "I hope this will help replace what he damaged."

Walking away, I wondered why I felt this strong sense of responsibility toward a dog I'd never spent time with? A dog that didn't even know me.

Because I knew his sisters so well, I felt I knew *him*, and for that reason, I figured I had the best chance of finding him.

As the days went by, fewer and fewer people turned up to look for Piki, but I knew it wasn't a question of how many looked for him: it would only take one to find him.

I've always found that a positive thought: you don't have to be loved by a lot of people; it only takes one.

It was now the end of August. No one else in the area seemed to have seen Piki. I had a friend who bred and trained Golden Retrievers and one of her dogs, Chukker, was a champion tracker. I told Katherine Piki's sad story and asked if she and Chukker would be willing to check the clusters of dog tracks we'd found to confirm if they were Piki's. She agreed, and we arranged to meet at 5:30 on the Sunday morning of Labor Day weekend. At that hour there would be less activity and fewer distractions

We drove together, as Katherine was in her late seventies and didn't have endless energy. We started near the home of the irate vacuum cleaner woman, hoping that Piki might have continued to visit. Her poor bulldog obviously never ran loose, so any tracks leading into and away from the fence might be Piki's. From these, Chukker might be able to get Piki's scent.

From that yard, Chukker followed tracks invisible to our eyes back across to the west side of the highway and down the wide forest trail where I had first seen the rope marks and fir cones. This eventually led to the well house on the computer mogul's property.

Trees had recently been cleared around the well house, and pressure sensitive lights had been installed. The ground was still muddy from the work, and we could see fresh dog tracks everywhere. We were certain we had found one of Piki's principal haunts. Pleased with ourselves, Katherine and I sat a nearby fallen log to reward ourselves with a break. It was still very early and so quiet that we didn't realize how close we were to a neighboring house and its driveway. We were just savoring coffee poured from a thermos when a man burst out the door, shouting in our direction.

"What are you doing on my property?"

"Sorry, sir." I was flustered. "We didn't know we were on your property. We didn't mean to trespass. We were just taking a break from tracking a stray dog."

We introduced ourselves. Softening, he replied, "I'm Nick Schaefer. I'm on my way to early church."

In our brief time together, Nick remarked that years ago he had been a member of one of the first teams on the island that tracked with dogs.

As we talked, it became clear that he was definitely a dog person, and he was becoming more sympathetic to our cause.

Since he was in a hurry, I blurted out my questions: "I live on the north end, twenty miles from here. Thanks to Chukker's work, we know that those are Piki's tracks around the well house. If you would be willing to feed Piki, I'll provide food, with bowls for food and water. Could you keep them filled? We need someone to keep an eye out for him. Any chance you could let us know if and when you see him?"

"I'll do whatever I can. It would be better, though, if you had a live trap we could feed him in."

We exchanged names and phone numbers. I promised to return the next day with dishes and a big bag of dry dog chow. And I said I'd look for a trap.

The next day, Labor Day, I left the supplies with Nick, who agreed to place them up near the well house. That way if Piki came to feed at night, he would trip the pressure lights and Nick would be able to watch him from his bedroom window.

I still had some time, and since there was quite a bit of holiday activity going on, I walked around the neighborhood. Finding small parties of people, I told them about Piki: "His name is Pikachu. Rhymes with *peekaboo*. He's medium-sized. A young black dog with white toes on each foot. Very skinny. Very shy."

People said things like "we haven't seen him around here," and "we'll keep our eyes open."

I asked everyone to notify the animal shelter if they did see Piki. I told one man about Piki's jumping a fence to play with a bulldog's toys and then running away.

"He sounds smart as a whip to me," the man said. "That's just the kind of dog I'd *like* to have."

Hearing this, I was as pleased as if Piki had been my own dog.

The trap my friend had loaned me to try to catch Starmie, the runt of the litter, was too small for her considerably larger brother. It took me a while to find a bigger one. I phoned the State Department of Wildlife and asked to be put in touch with a bear trapper. The trapper turned me down flat, saying that no bear trap could ever properly be rid of the smell of a dog, no matter how well it was cleaned up or how long ago the dog had been in it.

I got the name and phone number of a man sanctioned by Island County to control the island coyote population—in other words, to shoot them. He laughed at my hand-wringing concern for a stray dog and told me, "You can forget about using my trap."

It would be expensive to buy a trap large enough for Piki, and afterward it would take up a lot of storage space. I wasn't at all sure I wanted to own such a trap. If I did, I might have to end up trapping everyone's lost dog.

I presented my dilemma to Jill, the shelter manager, and she succeeded in arranging for a trap I could use indefinitely. I hauled it down to Nick's, and he went right to work, tightly wiring the door wide open, so that Piki would get used to going in and out with trust.

Nick also started to feed Piki by putting the food dish just inside the door. It was getting dark much earlier now, and he didn't have to wait long for Piki to show up. The well-house lights blinked on, and Nick watched as Piki suspiciously approached the trap. Like any teenage male, Piki was *hungry*. He tentatively sniffed the dog chow, gulped it down, and quickly retreated.

Elated, Nick phoned me. "It's him, all right. And he's eating the food and drinking the water. I don't know where he goes after the lights go out. By the way, he doesn't have a rope on him anymore."

Gradually, over the next few weeks, Nick moved the food dish farther inside the trap so that Piki would actually have to walk on its scary wire floor. Famished, the dog did whatever it took to get the food, though as soon as he finished eating, he quickly backed out of the trap.

The lights began to blink more frequently, often in the middle of the night, and Nick could see that Piki was eating from a bowl placed on the spring platform, all the way at the far end from the trap door. It was working as we had hoped.

On the last Sunday afternoon in September, Nick phoned to say that he planned to remove the wires that night and let Piki spring the trap.

We were both nervous. I could hear tension in Nick's voice, and for the rest of the day I couldn't think about anything else. I don't know if I even made dinner that evening. I just kept hoping and praying that the catch would be quick—and successful.

Then it struck me: what will we do once we have him? Piki could spring the trap within the hour. Or it could happen in the middle of the night. From the time Nick phoned me to say he had Piki, it would take me some thirty minutes to get there by car. Then we would have to load the trap in my car, and I would have to take Piki to the animal shelter. And the animal shelter was locked up and off limits from 5:00 p.m. until 8:00 a.m.

I rushed to the phone to call the shelter manager at home. I told her Nick's plan to spring the trap that night and that *if* we got Piki, I'd have to bring him to the shelter. Jill agreed to meet me at the shelter at any time during the night. I promised to let her know the outcome as soon as possible.

Relieved, I waited for Nick's call, not daring to go farther than inches from the phone. It was still early, around 8:30 p.m., when Nick called. His voice was strained: "He backed out."

"What?"

"When the door started to close, the metal made a squealing sound. Piki got so scared he just left the food, backed out, and ran like hell."

"Oh. My. God."

VII.

No Easy Answers

October – December 2000

Piki never came near the trap again.

Nick continued to put out bowls of food and water, but he placed them several yards away from the trap, instead of inside it. The food was eaten, but there was no point in keeping the trap. After about ten days I removed it and returned it to the shelter.

The October rains started: mists and drizzles at first, but later in the month, wind-driven rain in slanted sheets. Our house on the cliff above the sea shook, and the windows rattled. We began our annual winter worry about the roof blowing off.

Early in the month darkness was complete by six o'clock at night. Fingers of fog probed the open land unprotected by trees. The temperature dropped into the forties by day and on cloud-covered nights. On clear nights it was colder.

When I let our then family dog, Blue, out into the yard at night, I would stand and wait for him at the deck door, wondering where Pikachu was and how he was faring—cold, wet, hungry, lonely?

I felt awful.

There was nothing I could do for Piki until I thought of something new. My only hope and plan had been dashed.

I continued to work with Starmie and Jigglypuff. As I brought Starmie back to the shelter from a walk one cold, wet fall day, the idea hit me to warm a bath towel in the microwave oven and rub her dry before I put her back in her kennel. I never saw any creature so grateful for the warmth, the special attention, and the affection of that act. Covered from nose to tail by the warm towel, Starmie wiggled with pleasure and twisted her body into a half-moon. She snuggled under the cloth.

It proved to be a breakthrough. Hard as it may be to believe after all our months of interaction, neither Jigglypuff nor Starmie had ever greeted me by wagging their tails. From that time on, Starmie wagged me *hello.*

One afternoon I loaded Starmie into my car and drove to Oak Harbor. I wanted to give her a lesson in how to be with children. She always got motion sickness in my car, but that day I had the time to clean up after her. I thought that if she rode often enough, it might become less stressful for her and she might get over her carsickness.

I parked just beyond the limits of an elementary school where kids who walked and biked to and from school would be sure to pass by. The closing bell rang, the students poured out of the building and, in twos and threes, many of them approached where Starmie and I waited on the sidewalk. I squatted down low, close and protective to Starmie, at children's height, and with my hands on Starmie to reassure her from the scary onslaught.

"Oh, what a pretty puppy!"

"Can I pet her?"

"What's her name?"

The kids grabbed for Starmie. She cowered behind me. I stood up, towering over them, and said, "Yes, you can pet her, but you have to do it in a special way."

My simple act of standing up changed the relationship of from that of "pals" on the same level to that of adult versus child. Starmie sat nervously behind my legs. I squatted again, this time behind her, so that she couldn't move away. I held her under her chest and rear end.

"One at a time, you can come over and touch her, very gently."

A little girl reached over and patted her back.

"Oooh, she's so soft!" Surprised and successful, she stroked her again.

"She's a special dog," I continued, "and she's never been with kids before, so she's a little afraid."

"Awwww."

"*I* won't hurt her."

One by one, the little boys and girls petted Starmie.

Starmie loved it. Trembling at first contact, she soon settled down and enjoyed the attention.

"What's her name?" one boy asked.

"Starmie."

I thought I was going to have to explain the Pokémon names, as I always had to with grownups, but these kids just began to giggle. The name passed through to the kids in back, and, quickly, the giggle became laughter and shouts of delight.

"Starmie!"

They all knew Pokémon, and they were all about the same age as the young son of the shelter employee who had inspired the litter's name.

Seeing their delight, I added, "And she has a sister named Jigglypuff and a brother named Pikachu."

The youngsters were thrilled. Starmie couldn't possibly have scored more points with this young crowd. With smiling faces, they lingered until every one of them had had at least one chance to touch Starmie. After they went on their way, I put a very tired, happy Starmie back into my car and returned her to the shelter.

Several days later, hoping for the same success with Jigglypuff, I sat the two of us outside the Coupeville Elementary School as the students streamed out in the afternoon.

We bombed.

The first little girl who approached lunged at Jigglypuff. The dog was so frightened and the child so incorrigible that we had to leave. I put Jigglypuff back in the car and spent about an hour trying to calm her down before I took her back to the shelter. Difficult as this was, Jigglypuff must have realized how much I cared for her and had tried to protect her. From about this time on, I could hear the thump of her tail on the walls of her kennel when she saw me coming down the hall toward her.

In early October Jigglypuff spent a gorgeous Sunday afternoon at home with me. For a while I worked in the garden with her beside me on a long lead. Then I brought her inside the house, still on lead, and had her lie down beside Curt while he watched a football game on television and read the Sunday paper. On the way back to the shelter, I took her for a little stroll on the lovely old fire road at Fort Ebey State Park, entering through the back way that the locals use from their adjoining neighborhood.

When we reached the end of the short road, we heard unseen voices from not far away, people laughing and talking, the sound of campfire wood snapping as it burned. Jigglypuff panicked, turned around, and started back. Because she was so frightened, I humored her and turned with her. Then we ran smack into two people walking toward us. Beside herself, Jigglypuff ran circles around me, tying me up with her long leash, and when I tried to take a step forward, I fell at her feet, scraping my knees. The walkers rushed forward to see if I was hurt, and the dog almost dragged me off. I wasn't hurt, but the moment certainly clarified her disabling fear of being anywhere near strangers.

Once we were back in the car en route to the shelter, I was searching for something to listen to on the car radio when I stumbled on a call-in show devoted to solving problems with pets. The talk show hostess sounded competent and seemed to have a sincere interest in her clients' problems. It was a live show, and she had a veterinarian who was renowned in our region with her as a guest commentator.

I had never had the slightest inclination to participate in a radio talk show, so I debated for a few minutes whether or not to make the call. But what did I have to lose? I parked in front of a phone booth on Main Street in Coupeville, found some change, and placed the call. I told a call screener about my problem with Piki, and the screener seemed to find it interesting and unusual. Would I hold, please?

I didn't have long to wait before I repeated Piki's situation on the air. The commentator and the veterinarian consulted and talked over the problem. Piki had been petted and touched at the shelter, so he was technically not a full-fledged feral dog. But he had never been adequately socialized; he was terrified of men, children and everything not previously experienced; he had barely escaped from a humane trap and now could no longer be baited with food or water.

I could only hear what they said on the phone, not on the radio. After a few minutes the commentator announced, in a noticeably gloomy voice, that Border Collies were unusually nervous and intelligent dogs, and that, in the opinion of both herself and the vet, it would be almost impossible to catch this one and, if I did catch it, equally impossible to civilize the dog.

As I hung up the phone, I felt even more dismal about the situation with Piki than I had before I called.

I did, however, keep wondering: wasn't there something more we could do for this poor lost dog? When I received my fall newsletter from the Humane Society of the United States (HSUS) I decided that with my annual contribution, I would ask for the organization's help. A man at the HSUS office in California listened sympathetically and said, "I have just the person for you." He suggested I talk with a man named Lee LeBeau, who, he said, had caught many feral dogs and would be able to give me some good tips.

I called Lee and explained the problem of Piki's backing out of the trap. Lee sympathized greatly and made a suggestion that I realized immediately wouldn't work for me. His idea was to fence in a fair-sized area with wire and a gate, put food and water in a specific location within the fence, and then monitor the area day and night waiting to make friendly contact with the dog.

He was trying to be helpful and I could tell that his concern was sincere, but, as I explained to him, I lived some twenty miles away from where the dog was, had a husband and house to look after, and couldn't curl up indefinitely in a sleeping bag on the site, as Lee himself had done.

In mid October a young Navy couple appeared at the shelter, shopping for a dog. Someone showed them Starmie. They sounded like reasonable prospects for Starmie because while stationed in Naples, Italy, they had found a homeless and starving street dog that they adopted and brought back to the States with them. This pet dog had recently died, and now they were looking for another. Because they had already dealt with a dog who was a project, all concerned assumed that they would have the patience necessary to work with the very challenging Starmie. To their credit, this couple took time to think over this dog adoption, and they returned to the shelter several times to try to get to know Starmie.

This gave me an opportunity to speak with them. I wanted them to benefit from my knowledge of her. I printed out a three-page blurb I had written about my experiences with Starmie: her escape in the park, the episode with the school kids, her stress-related car sickness, and her various strengths and weaknesses. I encouraged them to anticipate situations that were new to her. This information went home with them when they adopted Starmie in late October.

I should have felt more joyful about Starmie's new family. I accused myself of being overly protective. I kept telling myself that I couldn't, shouldn't try to control "my" babies once they went into the hands of others. But, in my gut, I didn't like the brush-off that this couple had given my efforts to share my experience of Starmie. They'd folded the paperwork neatly, put it away and—I was almost certain—never read it. They had had one especially difficult dog, and they expected Starmie to be exactly the same. They knew how to handle this.

Nick Schaefer phoned me again around the second week in November. He was continuing to set out dry dog food, but it was no longer being eaten regularly. Also, the uneaten food was being scattered around the area of the dishes.

When Piki was eating the food, there was never any left.

Nick had a clever idea. He was going to lightly scatter white flour around the food bowls and examine any footprints that were left. He'd be able to see if it was raccoons getting the food as they have very distinctive paw prints. Unfortunately, the paw prints proved to be so mixed and unreadable that nothing conclusive was ever established.

But it did seem clear that Pikachu was gone, so we stopped the feeding.

During the howling gales of November, I stood nightly at the deck door thinking of Piki. When I awoke during the night, I would lie awake for hours mentally envisioning what I would do if I ever had a chance to catch him.

After eight months of almost daily attention to one, two, or all three of the remaining Pokémon puppies, I was down to a single dog—Jigglypuff—and her prospects were not all that promising.

Curt and I had long before planned a two-week vacation in Mexico at the end of November. I still visited and walked Jigglypuff regularly until we left, but I also turned my attention to preparing for our trip. It was a relief to have something besides these dogs to think about and wonderful to find myself in sunshine and warm sand. While I swam and walked along the beaches of Mexico, I had hardly a thought about life in dripping, dark, cold Washington State.

We returned in early December, the time when every mother and grandmother begins preparing feverishly for that extravagant production known as The Holidays. It was mid-month before I made it back to the shelter to check on Jigglypuff.

Ka thunk. Ka thunk. That tail hitting the wall of her kennel sounded like a heartbeat. And it was racing because she knew I was there. I went straight to her kennel without even looking at any of the other dogs.

She was delighted to see me, and I felt harpooned by guilt. I should have come before. Dogs never forget—their pleasure or their pain.

Jigglypuff and I hugged and kissed. She was more demonstrative than I had ever seen her: wagging, jumping, licking my face like any normal dog.

After a few minutes of happy reunion we ran the line of jealous, barking, agitated dogs and left the shelter on our walk. In spite of a cold, soaking rain; a muddy, pot-holed road; a landscape of ruined and rusting refrigerators; a mountain of scrap metal, I found it wonderful to be walking together, Jigglypuff by my side. No longer did I have to drag her behind me.

When I returned Jigglypuff to her kennel, I couldn't believe my eyes: was that Starmie in the kennel nearby?

Starmie!

Her tail rapidly beat the metal sides of her kennel.

Starmie was supposed to be living happily-ever-after with the Navy couple she'd been adopted by in October. What was she doing back at the shelter?

I entered Starmie's kennel and sat with her for a few minutes, getting the same warm and wet welcome from her that I'd gotten from Jigglypuff. Then I rushed to the office to hear what had happened.

Jill told me. It was almost exactly what had happened with her brother Pikachu. A short time after their adoption of Starmie, the Navy couple had left the dog alone in their car in a parking lot on the Navy base. It was a busy weekend day. Cars were parked close together, and people brushed by the nervous dog as they got in and out of cars and loaded groceries. It must have been too much for Starmie. We never found out how the dog escaped, but that's what she did.

Her adopters never informed the shelter that Starmie was gone. In the next several weeks some people noticed a stray dog hanging around Seaplane Base buildings in that quandary of an animal living on its own—hoping to be noticed, afraid to be noticed. No food was available to her in this area, and there was little shelter from the wild winter weather.

This hangout was not far from the city of Oak Harbor animal shelter, and that's where Starmie first went. I think she was probably so hungry that she willingly entered the live-trap that the city shelter manager set out for her.

The city shelter had a five-days-in-and-out—forever out—policy. That's the time clock Starmie was on when the county shelter manager, visiting on business, noticed and recognized the dog. Quietly, Jill arranged to take Starmie back to the county shelter on a dog exchange, never mentioning Starmie's long history there.

So, now Starmie was back, full circle, at the county shelter after her second and much more perilous escape.

In that moment I would have adopted the Pokémon puppies myself. But all of them? And if not that, then which one? I didn't know. Whichever one needed me the most.

After having seen Spike, I still had a hope that the right person could provide a home for Starmie and Jigglypuff—could, in other words, work a miracle with these sweet dogs.

I didn't hold much hope for Piki.

Part Two

Piki: A Cliff-Hanger

VIII.

Reconnecting

Once the feverish activity of the holidays was under control, my thoughts turned to the new year—and Pikachu. I remembered hearing that, sometime during the last busy months, the shelter had received a call from an angry woman in the Teronda West subdivision of Central Whidbey. She was complaining about a stray black dog that had appeared out of nowhere to bother her own dog when she was out walking him. Her description fit Piki, although the location was about a mile south of where he had been before.

I wasn't anxious to go jousting for a cause that had been so comfortably out of sight for some time now. Yet no one else was stepping forward on Piki's behalf, so a few days before Christmas, I contacted the shelter manager to obtain this woman's phone number. Then I waited a few more days to work up the courage to call this unknown—and angry—person. I phoned her finally on the Sunday afternoon of New Year's Eve.

"Yes, I'm the one who called about the black dog."

"Do you still see him?"

"Why, yes, he lives on the lot next door to me."

I was floored. "If this is a shelter dog that escaped from its owner in Bon Air last August, he doesn't like to get very close to people. Have you been able to see if he has white toes on all four feet?"

"Yes, he does." She explained that the dog would come right up to pester her little dog when they were out walking. "He got close enough for me to see him," she said, "but he would have nothing to do with me."

"Sounds just like Pikachu. He loves other dogs."

"Well, my dog is dead now."

I gulped, hoping the next thing she would say wasn't that Piki had in some way caused her dog's death.

"My little terrier was fifteen," the woman said, "and in poor health. It made him nervous when the black dog appeared out of nowhere. I didn't know if that skinny, hungry dog was a threat to him."

"Probably just wanted to play with him."

"It didn't look that way. But it doesn't matter anymore."

I thought this would be the end of the conversation, but the woman went on.

"I set food out for that dog every night now. What did you say his name was?"

"Pikachu. Rhymes with *peekaboo*."

A pause.

"How nice of you to feed him."

"Well, he's just skin and bones. I never see him eat it, but the food is always gone in the morning. Every bit of it."

This would explain his move from Nick Schaefer's location.

"You said Piki lives next door to you?"

"Yes, I can see him clearly from my rear deck.

Another longer pause. I hardly dared to breathe: she sees him!

"I only have to whistle for him to come out, and he sits on the edge of my backyard."

Instead of being mad at him, she has actually transferred her nurturing to an unwanted dog! I had been expecting difficulty and anger: I got nice.

Trying to contain my excitement, I asked, "Would it be all right if I drove down to see you both early tomorrow afternoon?"

"By all means. I'll be expecting you."

At a New Year's Eve party that night, I told a sympathetic friend that I was going to try to once again make contact with the elusive semi-feral dog I'd been concerned about for months.

"Chicken livers," he said. "When I was a boy, I trained a dog by rewarding him with small pieces of chicken liver that my mom cooked up for me."

"Wow," I said. "Those chicken livers must have been irresistible."

"Absolutely irresistible." He chuckled.

The next day dawned sunny: a promising beginning to the new year. I was itching to head south, but we had accepted an invitation to a brunch that morning. Besides, I had to cook all the chicken livers I had ferreted out of my freezer. As early as I could break away, I drove the twenty miles to the home of Margaret Sloan.

Identifying myself as yesterday's caller, I explained that I was a WAIF volunteer who was trying to catch Piki, get him out of the wild, and return him to the shelter.

Margaret was a weaver and a widow who, now that her dog had died, lived alone. She said that her neighbors had also encountered Pikachu when they were walking their own dogs. Nobody knew where he came from or to whom he belonged.

I filled Margaret in on Piki's shelter background, his sisters, the escape from his adoptive home, and his escape from the humane trap. I assured her that, like his sisters, he had a pure heart and that he was in no way a threat to her because he would rather flee than fight.

She seemed satisfied that I was committed to helping him and led me through her house to the back deck.

There, Margaret made good on her declaration. She whistled in the direction of the huge wild blackberry wall that protected Piki's fortress next door. Within seconds, a handsome black dog crawled to the end of a prickly tunnel, straightened up, and sat in the sunshine, facing Margaret's house.

My heavens! He had grown up in the months since I had last seen him. He was tall, raw-boned, gorgeous—and shockingly thin.

For a few minutes Piki basked in the warm sunshine. Margaret spoke to him in soothing tones. When I added my voice, Piki got up nervously and moved farther away. After a moment, he slipped back into hiding through a blackberry tunnel.

His audience for the day was over.

On January 2, I phoned Jill and reported the events of the previous day. WAIF volunteers and employees were delighted. Now we knew where and how to approach Piki. It had to be through other dogs.

For the next few days, two fellow WAIF volunteers brought their dog and I brought my own dog, Blue, to visit Piki. Blue was an eight-year-old love of a Golden Retriever/Australian Shepherd mix that Curt and I had adopted from WAIF almost exactly a year before.

Piki instantly made contact with the other dogs, but he was wary about the people. After months of having been shooed away by strangers, chased by young men trying to catch him, baited with offers of food and water, Piki sat at a distance and watched as Linda and Kari played Frisbee in front of him with their dog.

While the game was on, Blue and I checked out Piki's castle. Although the blackberry bushes were almost impenetrable on one side, there was an opening on another. Blue and I went into the bushes there and found a long-abandoned one-room house. The roof overhead was still mostly intact, so it was dry inside, but the wooden floor showed significant holes and wear. The windows and door were framed but had no fixtures. There was no furniture. The house had not been used in many years by anyone but Piki.

So this is where he spent those stormy winter nights!

After a few days Linda and Kari turned to other responsibilities and stopped coming. Blue and I continued because, of course, I had once again become completely absorbed: keeping in contact with Piki was now my highest priority. To do so, however, meant sacrificing time I would usually spend with Jigglypuff and Starmie. That's because if I worked with Piki, I had to bring Blue along with me, and if I worked with Piki's sisters, I would need to leave Blue in the car for long periods of time at the shelter. So, I had to juggle these various canine concerns in figuring out where to put my energy at this time. It was clear to me that Piki's need was the greatest.

Consequently, I never got to say goodbye to my beloved Jigglypuff. When I did finally make time to work at the shelter the next week, I found out that Jigglypuff had been adopted two days before, on January 4th. I rejoiced for her, but I also worried that her new owners would find her too weird and not have the patience they needed to have if she were going to learn to trust them.

It was, however, a miracle that she'd been adopted, and I was amazed about this sudden interest in her after so many months.

When I asked about the details, I found that Jigglypuff and her sad story had been featured in a scrapbook of adoptable animals made by a volunteer and circulated on the island. Gratified, I had just returned to work in the dog kennels when a beautiful young woman approached me and asked where she could find Jigglypuff. I told her Jigglypuff had been adopted and found that this woman had seen the same scrapbook and was also touched by Jigglypuff's story. Her disappointment seemed genuine to me, and as she turned to leave, I asked her, "Is Starmie featured in that book too?"

"Starmie?"

"Starmie is a littermate," I told her, "and an almost exact copy of Jigglypuff in every way." I led this young woman to Starmie's kennel and then, not wanting to appear possessive or overly hopeful, I left the two of them alone to get to know each other. I went into the office and told Jill that now, miraculously, someone might be interested in adopting Starmie as well. Jill had talked with the young woman earlier and told me that she was Louise Pierson, an old friend, a former WAIF volunteer, and an excellent and caring animal person. I was almost overcome with hope.

Louise went back home to think over the possibilities—and returned the following day, January 7, to adopt Starmie.

For the next several days I would begin my search for Piki in Teronda West by knocking on doors, talking to residents, asking about Piki's habits and haunts, and trying to establish my own credibility in the neighbors' eyes. I wanted them to know that when Blue and I prowled around their neighborhood, our motivation was to try to help Piki.

At one point I was sitting in the backyard of a sympathetic off-duty fireman, telling him Piki's story, and as if on cue, Piki trotted into the yard to play with this man's dog. The two dogs sniffed and wrestled, ran, jumped, and enjoyed playing until the fireman stood up. Piki seemed to perceive the man's rising as a threat and instantly bolted from the yard. The other dog couldn't follow because he wore a collar that confined him to his yard, using an electric signal coordinated with an underground electric invisible fence.

Piki's fondness for other dogs was confirmed around the neighborhood. Several other neighbors reported seeing Piki inside their fenced yards, playing with their dogs and with their dogs' toys, eating their dogs' food, even sleeping in their doghouses with them.

One woman said she'd gotten up in the middle of the night recently to check how her Rottweiler in the back yard was faring in the cold. She was surprised to see how large he looked, lying asleep on the deck. The super-sized black lump turned out to be two black lumps—Piki cuddling up with her Rottie, the two of them staying warm together.

Lara, another neighborhood resident I approached, was able to vouch for my honesty with her neighbors because she and I both knew about a woman killed in a motorcycle accident on North Whidbey the previous summer. This unfortunate woman had left behind an orphaned litter of valuable young Belgian Tervuren puppies. Lara and I compared notes about the community scramble to care for those pups and this shared knowledge convinced Lara that I was who I said I was: a WAIF volunteer hoping to catch Piki and return him to the shelter.

Everyone that I talked to in the neighborhood was interested in finding out who Piki was, why he was there, and what I was hoping to do about him.

Blue and I were making direct progress with Pikachu. Each day, I would park at Margaret's, our home base, and I would walk Blue on leash around the neighborhood. Periodically we stopped and I gave him a deliciously smelly chicken liver treat from a little plastic bag I carried in my pocket. Piki didn't take long to appear, running up to Blue, sniffing and nuzzling him, and walking along near us. After he watched Blue eat, I'd pitch a piece of liver on the ground for Piki. He acted suspicious at first but found the chicken liver as predicted: irresistible. I always talked softly to Blue in a pleasant voice, describing what was going on, what I was doing, what I was hoping to do—all to get Piki used to the sound of my voice.

Within a couple of days I was able to feign indifference to Piki, turning my head away from him while extending my arm full-length to see if he would take a treat from my hand. He did— as long as I wasn't looking directly at him. A few more days and we got to the point where I could squat down and feed him from my extended arm while making eye contact with him. Then he skittered away.

Piki seemed to be trapped in a dog limbo—unable to fully commit to life either with or without people.

Years before when I had my first experience with a feral cat, I'd learned that it was vital to break off contact when the cat was enjoying it the most— to always leave the animal wanting more, eager for your return; never, ever let *the animal* walk away from *you*. For this reason, my meetings with Piki were relatively short, especially when you consider the length of time it took me to pack the chicken livers and Blue, and drive the forty-mile round-trip.

So that I could reach additional people, Margaret Sloan arranged for me to attend a neighborhood association meeting scheduled on the morning of January 8. The group included about a half-dozen friendly middle-aged women and one unpleasant old man. I described Piki's history and situation and asked for the community's cooperation until I could catch this stray and return him to the shelter. The women nodded their assent. The man stood abruptly and said, "When I see that black dog-pound-son-of-a-bitch, I'll shoot him. I'm going to get out my rifle, and I'm going to tell my neighbors to get theirs out, too.

The shock in the room was palpable. The women looked at one another as if there were no point in saying anything. There certainly wasn't for me. I left, knowing I had limited time to save Piki. There it was: the old saw that says extermination is the solution to any problem.

The next afternoon was chilly and drizzly, and the chicken livers ran out early. Piki returned to his dry house and went inside. I didn't know what to do. It was too early to just pick up and drive back home, but how could I best spend the time I still had—especially with the added pressure of knowing someone was possibly gunning for my baby?

Blue, Piki, and I had always done something active before, but this time I sat down in the tall, wet grass about twenty feet from the open doorway of Piki's house and called Blue. Blue sat on my left, and I began to stroke him, singing softly all the while. Blue melted down and lay in front of me, silver droplets of drizzle collecting on his beautiful long brown and black hair. I pretended not to notice Piki, but I was inwardly shocked when he volunteered to come out of his house. Out of the corner of my eye, I saw him lie down on my right side about six feet away. Just out of reach, but close enough for me to notice a pink blister of skin about the size of a fingernail between two toes on his right front foot.

Amazed by Piki's coming close and afraid to break the moment, I hardly stopped for breath. I continued quietly singing; humming; whistling slow, gentle songs; and keeping my hands on Blue. Piki actually closed his eyes and relaxed—although he lay like a sphinx, with his head up and forelegs out in front of him, ready to spring to his feet in a nanosecond. He seemed to be enjoying this quiet, calm interlude. It was the first time I'd ever seen him in such a tranquil state.

Was this what he'd been wanting? Quiet time? Coming to a full stop? Did this dog just want to lie down and be petted?

Piki had had some loving physical contact with volunteers, especially women, petting him at the shelter. Could he possibly be motivated by the desire for loving human touch, the desire for calm and for someone to trust?

IX.

Capture

On Wednesday, January 10, I arrived in Teronda West in the mid afternoon, my pockets loaded with bags of cooked chicken livers and a worn tennis ball in hand. Instead of just walking the neighborhood with Blue on lead, this time I played throw-and-retrieve with Blue on the north side of Margaret's house, adjoining Piki's blackberry patch fortress. He soon came out to watch, fascinated.

Having never played the kinds of games that humans normally play with their dogs, Piki didn't join in. Finally exhausted, big Blue gave up the game, came to me, lay down and rolled over for a belly rub. I buried my face in his hairy chest, blew hot-breath bubbles to amuse him and stroked his long, luxurious black and brown hair. Curious, Piki came closer, close enough to smell Blue's crotch while he was lying on his back. Only an arm's length away, I was tempted to reach for Piki to try to pet him, too. But I didn't. This was what I had lain awake all those long, dark nights thinking about.

There must be no false moves. I had to have his trust. I was going to have only one chance to capture him and it was going to have to be fail-proof.

Blue and I got up and wandered around the yard. Piki moved with us. Blue found something interesting to smell a few yards away, and Piki sat down in front of me. My gut feeling told me that he wanted to be petted, that just as I had touched Blue affectionately, Piki actually *wanted* me to touch him. I squatted next to him on his right side. He didn't move away. I touched his white chest with my right hand and lightly drew small circles on it with my index finger.

At last he was getting the attention he craved, with no strings attached. I put my left hand on his back and when he didn't object, moved it around to pet his left shoulder. Was this going to be the moment when I should try to catch him? Or should I settle for just touching him now and hope he would allow me to pet him again sometime in the future?

I thought of the armed and angry old man in the neighborhood meeting.

Piki still wore the now-faded purple nylon collar he'd had on when he was adopted five months before. It was uncomfortably tight, but not yet ingrown. The D ring sewn into it was still intact and strong. Petting him with my left hand strongly enough to keep his attention, I used my right hand to quietly, slowly undo the knotted leash tied around my waist. Then I guided the hook end of the leash through the hand loop to make a slipknot. Piki was finally letting down his guard enough to enjoy the pleasure of warm touch and human contact.

I slowly took a deep breath. Still petting, and maintaining the slipknot, I gently attached the hook end of the leash into the D ring of his collar, keeping the leash slack. After a moment of disbelief that this had actually worked, I quietly slipped the other end, the lasso, over his head, not yet allowing it to tighten. I returned to petting Piki with my right hand, though it still gripped the leash, as well as my left.

I had him.

I was trembling. Time had stood still, but now I noticed that daylight was fading. I looked at my watch: 4:30. The shelter closed at 5:00.

Now I had to get Piki into the car!

I called Blue, and he ran to me. My legs were stiff from squatting so long, and it took me a moment to unfold and stand up. As I did, the now-shortened leash tightened, and Pikichu realized he was caught.

Like a bucking horse, Piki burst forward, straining from side to side, fighting to get away, yanking at the leash, almost disjointing my arms. I braced my legs and pulled the struggling dog in the opposite direction, toward the car, straining my every muscle. The mood had abruptly changed, and Blue, now wild-eyed with excitement, danced around us both on the way to the car, not knowing what to make of our struggle.

I finally dragged Piki over to the car and was briefly able to hold his leash with one hand so I could open the car door for Blue, who stood there for a moment, hesitant to get in. I yelled at him, and he jumped in. The rear seats were folded in the down position for Blue's convenience because we seldom needed them for human passengers.

Piki would *not* voluntarily follow Blue into the car. No wonder. He had only been in a car two other times—when he was delivered as a puppy to the shelter and when he was adopted—and for him neither of these was a happy day.

Struggling with my bulky, oversized parka, I tried to back through the rear door and drag Piki into the car with me. Piki strained and struggled with all his might to go in the other direction. In the midst of this, Blue, who hated conflict of any kind, decided he would be better off in the front passenger's seat and squeezed right over the top of me to get into it.

At last I dragged Piki into the back seat with me and, holding him tight, reached around him to pull the rear door shut. Success! I was breathing hard. Sweat poured out of me. I was exhausted. And time was flying by.

I slipped out of my parka and left it in the back, squeezed between the seats into the front, pushed Blue over to the passenger's side, and fired up the engine. As I was backing out of Margaret's driveway, Pikachu, wild-eyed with fear, realized he was alone in the rear and bolted from the back into the front, landing between the steering wheel and me, on my lap. He liked it there, but he was not a lap-size dog. I forced him over to the passenger seat and tried to hold him there, dislodging Blue, who took refuge on the floor below. Blue looked up at me reproachfully.

With me in the driver's seat, Blue on the floorboards, and Piki held at arm's length in the front passenger seat, I drove—agonizingly slowly—through the subdivision and back toward the main highway. The gray twilight was darkening to charcoal. Once I turned onto the highway, I could step on the gas and try to speed the ten miles back to the shelter before it closed. I had a feeling that like the wild animals I hauled when I used to volunteer with the wildlife clinic, the dogs would settle down as soon as the car speeded up. I was right; they did. When the car speed reached fifty, Piki voluntarily left the overcrowded front seats and returned to the rear.

It was black-dark by the time we reached the shelter, but the gate between the highway and the parking lot hadn't yet been closed. From where my car was idling in the parking lot, I could see Patty working outside of the kennels, which were illuminated by the outdoor floodlights. I didn't dare risk opening a door and having Piki bolt out. I blinked the headlights at Patty. She waved back but didn't make any move to come toward me.

Of course not. It was just a car with blinking headlights. She had no idea who we were.

I beeped the horn. Now she stopped what she was doing and came over to our car. I let down the driver's side window an inch and said, "Look who I have here."

Patty saw the two dogs in the back, looked more closely, and quietly breathed, "Pikachu!" She paused for a moment. "Stay right where you are until I can get a kennel ready." And she dashed back inside.

When she returned, she told me, "Drive the car through the inside gate and follow me to the door in the fence. I'll close the gate behind you and have the kennel closest to the gate ready for him with the door open. We'll take him from the car into the kennel in a straight shot."

I stopped the car next to the door in the fence and quickly got out the driver's side door, fearful that Piki would jump over me to escape. He stayed in the back of the car with Blue. I left the front car door open to form a partial barricade while Patty stood by at the rear car door. I reached in through the driver's door and grabbed Piki's leash.

He had stopped fighting. I think he knew he was back at his long-time shelter home, and he was thinking that was not all bad. Patty and I led him out of the car, through the fence door, and into his kennel. I settled him on his bed, unhooked the leash and pulled the slipknot off his neck. I sat down on the cold, damp cement floor next to him and petted him while Patty filled his food and water dishes.

Finally, on this dark January evening, Piki settled down as if he were home. Maybe not free, but certainly with a roof over his head, dependable food and water, and the companionship he craved.

Shortly after I got home, I phoned Margaret Sloan to tell her I'd caught him.

Laughing and cutting me short, she said she'd watched the whole thing from her upstairs bathroom window. Knowing she couldn't help me, she didn't interfere.

X.

Return to the Shelter

January – April 2001

Just a few days after Piki's return to the shelter, the Martin Luther King, Jr., holiday made for a long weekend. Late that Saturday, I asked Jill's permission to take Piki home with me, just as I had often done with his sisters, Jigglypuff and Starmie. She agreed, and at closing time, I put him in the car with Blue. We were all curious to see how he would behave in a home environment. Since he was clearly unadoptable at this stage, there was no point in keeping him in the shelter to meet the people looking for dogs.

Shelter smells had masked Piki's doggy odor, but once we got into our house, it was apparent that he had lived for months outdoors. I took him outside to pee and then, keeping him on his leash, I took him directly into the shower with me to give him his first-ever bath. He acted amazed, but didn't fight it. In fact, he seemed to like the lukewarm water flowing over him.

When I had finished washing and rinsing him, Piki leaped out of the tub and, before I could get a towel on him, shook himself exuberantly. Water droplets flew all over the bathroom, spraying the floor, sink, walls—even the ceiling. I finally succeeded in throwing a bath towel over him and started blotting the water—first one towel, then two, then three. I dried myself and, still holding his leash, mopped up the water in the bathroom with the towels.

Leaving the bathroom a few minutes later, I put on pajamas and a robe, wrapped Piki in dry towels and, with him still on a leash, marched him into the family room. I picked him up and set him next to me on the couch, half on my lap. His body and the top of his head were swathed in bath towels, his legs immobilized by them. Piki dozed to the sound of television while my body heat and the heat of the room dried him. Curt kept a low profile in another part of the room, so Piki knew he had nothing to fear from that quarter.

That night I slept in the guest bedroom with the door closed so that the cats couldn't come in. I looped the handle of a twenty-foot leash around my ankle and the other end was hooked into Piki's collar. He awakened me several times during the night, the leash tugging on my leg, but when he discovered that he was not free to roam, he settled down and slept.

First thing in the morning, I took him outside in the back yard with Blue. Then, I fed both dogs, setting down the bowls in different rooms so that there would be no food-fighting issues. Piki was delighted to get a little canned dog food mixed in with dry dog chow. This was routine at our house, but a treat the shelter budget could seldom afford.

After breakfast, I led Piki around the inside of the house so that he could become familiar with the layout. We also formally introduced him, still on leash, to our three cats. Neither Puck nor Halo, our male feral cats, could care less about a new dog in the house. They paid little attention to Piki and soon wandered away. On the other hand, any new arrival would have to be cleared by Tessa for admittance. We had learned from her previous introduction to Jigglypuff not to arrange this meeting in a small, enclosed bedroom.

We waited in the living room, as Tessa strode in. I pushed Piki down to a sitting position and squatted behind him to block escape, one hand on his collar and the other petting his back, trying to calm him. He would have to tip me over to run away. His muscles tensed as Tessa approached. He trembled and tried to bolt, but I held him firmly in place.

The cat's nose sniffed the end of his tail, then his toes. He whined softly. Finally, she stood nose-to-nose with him.

Piki never growled or barked at the cat, never showed any aggressive behavior. All he wanted to do was to run away, to keep this cat far from him in any way possible.

After a moment of impasse, Tessa turned her back on the dog and strode away at a measured pace. Her job was done. She had tested Piki and found him to be, like his sister, a devout coward. From now on he would know his place in the house: as Tessa's underling. There being no further challenge for her here, the cat went on to other matters.

I took the dogs for a long morning walk, not letting Piki off the lead until after we'd re-entered the house. He napped within sight of Blue and slept fairly soundly, considering all the new smells, sounds, and sights of this strange place.

I planned to walk in a different location that afternoon, since I've always believed that going to various places and smelling interesting smells is mentally stimulating for dogs over and above the benefits of physical exercise. I intended to tire the dogs out, figuring it would be naptime again for them when we got home.

Around 3:30 I loaded the dogs into the car. Getting Piki to feel comfortable in the car was easier already. He was willing to do whatever Blue did, and Blue was a model of good behavior.

Guessing that Piki had never seen a large town or many cars in one place, I drove to the downtown area of our small city. When the traffic light ahead of us turned red and we had to wait, with cars idling close by on either side of us, Piki became frantic.

I heard the unexpected sound of running water, but the light turned green just as I turned to look for its source. Then, I didn't need to look: I smelled it.

Piki had peed uncontrollably over the blanket that I had spread out over the flattened rear seats. A gusher.

I cracked open the windows to lessen the smell and parked as soon as I could to roll up the blanket and get it out of the way.

Oh, Lord, would he ever learn to relax in new situations!

We drove into the old part of town where the buildings stood shoulder to shoulder and formed a shadowy canyon. The road narrowed. We had to go more slowly. Piki pawed and clawed at the seats, whining. For him, this was almost as scary as it could get.

I turned at the next corner and took a street that led out to open spaces near the harbor. Piki's fear meter dropped immediately.

That night we started with same sleeping arrangement as the night before, but because things were going reasonably well, and the cats were ignoring him, I got up during the night and let Piki off the lead. I heard him leave the bedroom and I lay awake for a while, listening, trying to figure out where he might be in the house. There was silence, no commotion, no confrontations, so I soon went back to sleep.

When I awoke in the morning and went through the kitchen into the dining room, I discovered how Piki had spent much of the rest of the night. There, in pieces on the floor, was the wreckage of one of my leather hiking boots, chewed into small bits.

It was my own fault. I should have anticipated it, but I hadn't.

On the Monday morning of the holiday, Curt joined me, Piki, and Blue on a walk in the woods at Fort Ebey State Park. Another drippy, drizzly day, but Piki was frisky and happy to be back among the tall trees.

Instead of the normal choke chain I put Piki into a prong collar—in case I needed to make more effective corrections—and on a long lead. Blue roamed ahead off-lead. Smells in the damp underbrush must have been tantalizing because Piki frequently plunged into the brush. After he did this several times, I went forward to the front of the leash to urge him back onto the path. Grasping the leash in my left hand, I put my right hand on Piki's back to get his attention. As I reached for his collar, I was shocked to see that one of the prong links had come loose and was about to part from the others. If I hadn't discovered it, we would have repeated Starmie's first escape: the collar would soon have dropped off and Piki would have been free —back to living in the woods again, in a new and more remote location, without having been with us long enough to establish any allegiance. A near miss.

I grabbed Piki and put him on the path, looping the leash around his neck and urging Curt to hurry up to us. I needed him to secure Piki with the rest of the leash while I reattached the prong in the collar to fix it.

With considerable relief, I returned Piki to the shelter later that day. He'd had his brief fling with family living, and we'd had our experience with a young adult dog fresh from the wilds, a dog who knew and cared little about us or family life. We all needed a breather.

Besides, Piki had another important reason to return.

When I had first brought back Pikachu to the shelter, the veterinary staff immediately spotted the small pink bulge of skin between two toes on his right front foot that I had seen the day I sang to him and Blue in the rain. It was a tumor, in an awkward place, and growing noticeably. It would have to be surgically removed and biopsied.

The surgery was performed within a day or two of Piki's weekend at our house. As soon as he recovered from the anesthetic, I went to visit him in his shelter kennel.

Piki looked pathetic. He rose to greet me and wagged his tail slowly, but his head was separated from the rest of his body by a large, white plastic Elizabethan collar that was fastened around his neck—a funnel-shaped cone designed to prevent him from licking his foot and tugging out the stitches. It extended twelve inches in every direction and completely changed his normal perceptions of depth and direction. Because the collar prevented peripheral vision, he bumped into everything.

And still, Piki tried to work at the stitches as much as possible, eventually getting one out.

We wanted to keep his foot as clean as possible, so he couldn't go outside. I sat on the floor next to his bed. He climbed into the bed, lying down and letting me pet him and talk to him for as long as I was willing to do so—all afternoon, every afternoon for the next week.

On the following Monday, January 22, when I went in, I was greeted by shelter staff members with long, gloomy faces.

"Oh, no, not Piki! There's nothing wrong with Piki, is there?" I said, my voice rising. We hadn't yet received his biopsy results.

"It's not Piki," one of the girls said. "We have bad news about Jigglypuff."

The pit of my stomach dropped.

"Jigglypuff was hit by a car yesterday. She didn't make it."

"How did it happen?" I asked, dazed. "Her new family seemed so certain they could handle anything that came up."

"They said she was out on the second-floor deck of their house with them around noon on Sunday. She got spooked by something, jumped off the deck and ran away. Sometime later that afternoon a sheriff's deputy came to their door with her collar and ID tags and told her family she'd been killed by a car."

My darling, quirky Jigglypuff: so soft and sweet and loving and weird. I remembered the thrill of the first time she wagged her tail for me—and how many months it had taken to get her to that point. Sadly, she hadn't had enough time with her new family to become accustomed to them, to be comfortable in their world. Now she was gone.

How very much alike the three dogs were. Pikachu, Starmie and Jigglypuff: all runners, all suffering the hardships of their flights. Each of them with a gentle nature and such positive qualities, each responsive to human touch and appreciative of it; yet each so fearful, choosing to flee before they could bond with those who would care for them.

XI.

The One Right Person

Then came some good news: Piki's biopsy was negative, the tumor not malignant.

Several of us at the shelter were worried that Piki's owners-for-a-day might somehow learn about his return and reclaim him. We decided to change his shelter name. Because he was becoming familiar with the sound of Piki, I suggested Pete, to keep the *ee* sound.

Jon, one of the most faithful shelter volunteers, just couldn't bring himself to call this dog Pete. He shuddered at the memory of another dog named Pete who had come into the shelter long ago. Jon could barely finish saying, "His owner had hit the dog in the head with a shovel."

We put the new name on Piki's kennel door, but continued privately to call him Piki. Most adopters soon change their new dog's shelter name, so it was really only a matter of record-keeping. In fact, taking the precaution of changing Piki's name proved unnecessary because his first adoptive family never tried to reclaim him.

While his incision was healing, a slow process, Piki had little to do but lounge inside the interior compartment of his kennel. The width of the Elizabethan collar did not permit him to exit through the small door to the outside area. This meant that he had to pee and poop within a few feet of his bed and food dishes. He hated that.

Having so little to do was also hard on him. After all, Piki was a rambunctious teenager. I sat with him inside his kennel every afternoon to help him pass the time. I petted him, spoke to him, sang to him. When he tried to bite the tightening stitches, I distracted his attention, catching his eye and talking to him. At the end of the day when I had to close the kennel door and leave him alone, I found I missed him—and fancied that he was sorry to see me go.

In a few weeks, Piki had healed, and we were able to remove the miserable plastic collar. That alone improved his morale. Then he was cleared to use the play yard—heaven!

I still visited him daily. We spent hours in the play yard. After he was able to walk on gravel comfortably and through mud puddles without risking infection, we took long walks around the dump. Eventually, Jill permitted me to take Piki off-campus again, both as a change of scene for him and to get him acquainted with new and more frightening stimuli: people, cars, walks in the nearby town.

On days when I was feeling bold, we went into Coupeville, a picturesque seaside town on Central Whidbey that draws lots of sightseers. Putting Piki on a long lead, I'd take him down to Penn Cove beach. He loved the water and went in as far as his lead allowed. For in-town strolling along Front Street, I kept him on a short lead. He was terrified by everything we encountered in the old-town commercial district: the pavement, the closely placed buildings, and especially the people. Spotting a tourist strolling a block away made Piki quiver with fear. When someone made direct eye contact or tried to touch him, Piki squirmed out of reach until he was safely behind me. These confrontations with civilization were such an emotional and physical strain for Piki—and thus for me—that we didn't go to Coupeville all that much.

More often, I drove to the beach at Ebey's Landing, directly west of the town, a conservation area where the northern reaches of Puget Sound meet the Strait of Juan de Fuca. It was much easier on Piki to be in nature.

I particularly remember one gray and drizzly February afternoon. We walked on the beach for a short while and, returning to the car, we sat together, Piki and I. We had plenty of time, and I didn't want to return him early to the noise and commotion of the shelter.

A low cloud ceiling blanketed the Olympic Mountains across the water. Small waves softly lapped the beach stones. Piki sat tall in the front passenger seat, dozing. His head was bowed and his neck gracefully arched, accentuating the bony bump at the top of his skull. This bump, more prominent in some dogs than others, is just a feature of the dog's skull, but is laughingly known by many as the Bump of Knowledge. Piki's bump was extraordinarily large for such a young dog, and I considered the many hard knocks he had endured to earn such a prominent prize.

I stroked him, speaking softly to him, and the still napping Piki breathed a long, deep sigh. It was the first time I had ever seen this dog relax completely—a very special moment for me. Piki was finally at ease in my presence.

We stayed there that afternoon, sitting in the car, until I had to get him back to the shelter.

Spring, with its sunnier skies and warmer weather, brought an increased number of prospective adopters to the shelter. It was the usual crowd. Shelter workers say that most people can look directly at a large, black mongrel and never even see the dog. Black is the least desirable color. As for size, they want small dogs. The next choice is purebreds or exceedingly handsome mixed-breeds with at least some training. As a last resort, they will consider a black, short-haired, mongrel with a white patch on its chest: the quintessential pound dog.

And for the rare person who troubled himself to even try to see Piki through the chain link fence of his outside kennel, this shy dog would immediately retreat through the small door dividing interior from exterior—and stay inside until the prospective owner gave up and moved on.

SHY PIKACHU PEEKING OUT OF SHELTER KENNEL

Disappointing as this behavior was, it protected Piki from one of the hazards dogs can experience in shelters—people sticking their fingers through the wire fencing and into the cages, provoking bites, for which the dog then pays with its life.

My caring for Pikachu was proving to be a mixed blessing. I was giving him the attention he craved in the hope that I would instill in him a trust for people so that he could become more adoptable. Starmie and Jigglypuff had found new homes; I thought Piki could as well. But what was happening was something else: Piki was growing dependent on me and didn't care to even try to make other human friends.

Once I realized this, I tried staying away from the shelter for a week to see if he behaved differently when I wasn't around. But he was more alone than ever, and perhaps lonelier now. He didn't solicit attention from the prospective adopters looking at him; shelter employees didn't have time to spend with him; other volunteers, also busy, considered Piki to be my project, not theirs. Being away from Piki was hard on me, and I think it was hard on him, too. Since no purpose was being served by my withdrawing, I returned to work with my favorite dog.

In March, Jill called a meeting of volunteers to hear a talk by an exuberant young woman from a local service dog organization. This group had been formed the year before to train and place therapy, mobility, and hearing assistance dogs.

It's my observation that dedicated volunteers of any newly formed organization are often certain their efforts are going to save the world. Dynamic and excited about her goals, this woman was no exception. She talked about how trainable dogs can be discovered in unexpected places and said she was scouring area animal shelters, looking for suitable prospects.

Certainly, she had a good audience for her message. Shelter employees and volunteers invariably warm to the idea that an otherwise unappreciated dog might get a chance to be trained and loved, and in turn, to be of service to someone in the community. All of us listening that day agreed to be on the lookout and report prospects to her organization.

I, however, spotted a few flaws in all of that boundless enthusiasm.

First, this woman talked at length about a dog she had recently found running unattended on Chuckanut Drive, a narrow and dangerous two-lane road on the mainland about twenty miles north of the northern end of Whidbey. It was a scenic destination with a sheer rock wall on one side and a sharp drop-off to railroad tracks and the ocean on the other.

She described how she'd stopped briefly to open the door of her car to get the dog off the road. The dog willingly jumped in. Finding no collar or identification tags, she drove on. Once she'd found a safe spot to get the out of the car, she saw that it was young, affectionate, smart, obedience-trained, and an altogether great candidate for training as an assistance dog.

I had to wonder who had done all of the earlier work on this wonderful dog. A dog like that very likely would have a loving owner waiting somewhere, worrying about his missing pet. Had this young woman put forth any sustained effort to report her newfound prize, allowing the dog to be reclaimed by its rightful owner? Or had she rested in her own certainties that this dog fit perfectly into her agenda?

Second, while this woman looked over the shelter dogs, I found some tasks to do that kept me at a discreet distance. I knew these dogs personally and knew they behaved differently outside their kennel doors. I knew that some of them had been well-loved and trained and had only reverted temporarily to dog-pound wildness that would soon again be overcome by gentle and loving care. I knew that some of their owners had reluctantly surrendered them because they suffered an economic downturn and others because they were being deployed overseas. Still others had withheld the truth or told outright lies about the dog's age, health, or aggressive behavior on the surrender questionnaire, thus passing on potential problems to the next adopter. I had to ask if this last ploy is any more than just a small step up from pushing the animal out of a car and abandoning it? Or locking it in a crate and dumping it outside the shelter before opening hours, both of which actions occur not infrequently.

This woman seeking potential service dogs spent only seconds in front of each kennel, sizing up the frenzied dogs she saw and rejecting them instantly. She didn't seem to understand that a shelter dog that sits quietly inside its kennel as a human looks at it is probably depressed.

I didn't expect this woman to dub Pikachu as a candidate for her training. As usual, he hid. But there were other dogs, exceptionally smart and loving dogs, that might have fit well into her program had they received a lengthier assessment and the benefits of the training. Why were they so summarily dismissed?

These dark thoughts began to swirl in my mind and, with them, I was making myself increasingly blue. When would the person come, The One Right Person who would take the time and trouble to recognize the potential intelligence and loving nature hidden within Piki's shy and easily spooked exterior? Who, besides me, would ever see the injustice of throwing away this strange and fearful dog, of writing him off just because it took a little extra effort to deal with him? It would take The One Right Person, indeed: someone willing to do the hard work of love.

Then, as if I were standing outside of myself as I listened to my internal conversation, the spectator in me realized that, in fact, I wasn't being quite honest with myself. I wasn't working to prepare Piki to live happily ever after with someone else. I myself wanted to be, and was, The One Right Person.

I had always told myself that if I could only take one of the remaining Pokémon trio, I'd choose the one who needed me the most. Now Jigglypuff and Starmie had found other homes. That left Pikachu.

I wanted him. He wanted me. I could be The One Right Person.

Now, if some other miracle person didn't come along for Piki, it became my task to get my other human half, my husband, to agree to take on this challenging dog.

XII.

The Decision

April 2001

In mid April, the shelter manager said, "Barb, I have to talk to you."

What Jill had to say was no surprise, though I was pleased that she managed to say it gently: "Piki just can't go on here as he is."

"I know. I know. When someone tries to look at him, he runs inside his kennel and hides until they move on."

"Worse yet. Most dogs that stay here as long as he has ultimately lose it."

She was right. This worst-case scenario was a possibility I'd never wanted to admit to myself: Piki could do what some other long-term shelter dogs had done: become mentally ill. It wasn't a pleasant prospect. But Jill wasn't trying to scare me; she had a solution to suggest.

"Jon has offered to take him."

I saw this as both good news, and bad. Jon was a valued, longtime shelter volunteer and a personal friend. He and his partner, Phil, owned extensive rural property on the south end of the island, where they took most of the unadoptable shelter canines. The dogs lived as a pack on this private, fenced land.

Jon and Phil were two of the kindest people I know. They provided food, water, bedding, shelter, and space. They did not, however—in contrast with my own viewpoint—believe in training these dogs. Indeed, they conscientiously refrained from imposing anything more than the most minimal human will upon these dogs. They believed that the dogs would sort out their own status, strong to weak, and live more happily being self-governed.

The approach seemed to work well until the top dog, a big Malamute, died. Then Metek, a young male purebred Siberian Husky I had worked with extensively at the shelter before he went to Jon's, challenged another young male to see which of them would become the new top dog. The fighting was intentional and vicious, the damage to each serious, and the result, to my mind at least, tragic. Metek had to be euthanized.

Metek had been painfully shy around people, but I thought he showed promise adjusting to human demands. I had not participated in the decision to send him to Jon's, and a short time later, he was dead. I didn't say anything about it to Jon, whom I liked and respected, but privately I saw it as a waste of a good dog.

Now Jon wanted to offer Pikachu a happily-ever-after home in the same pack. I knew Piki was capable of surviving in this situation because I felt he would rather run away or submit to another dog than fight. Yet I had the persistent feeling that he could do better. Piki was capable of learning to enjoy close contact with people. I felt certain that he could eventually adjust to new and unknown situations. He could, in short, become a trusting and touchable family pet.

I hesitated to accept Jon's offer to take Piki, and Jill knew me well enough to put forward another option.

For difficult cases the shelter worked with a canine obedience school near Seattle. The school would give a free evaluation of a dog's trainability. Jon and I were to take Pikachu to this facility and meet with Maureen, the owner and head trainer, who would tell us whether or not, in her judgment, Piki could be trained.

I snatched this option and agreed to abide by the trainer's judgment.

I told my husband, Curt, about the impending decision. My husband had been aware of the visits by Starmie and Jigglypuff, but his limited involvement with Piki's sisters had been mostly to take an occasional photograph of me with one of the dogs when I asked. Curt knew that these dogs were odd. He knew about my all-nighter when Starmie escaped in the park, and he knew too that I had been going to the shelter almost daily for a year to work with them and with Piki. But I had never asked him outright if we could adopt any of these dogs. Much as I had wanted any or all of them, I knew how much the arrival of such a dog in our home would upset our established way of life, and not briefly but for an indefinite—probably lengthy—time. I had maintained a hope for all of the dogs that they would be adopted by someone else, but Piki just couldn't wait any longer.

On the morning of our visit to dog training school Curt *did*, to my delight and surprise, suggest that Piki could come to live with us. I think he said this because he felt secure that the trainer would decide that Piki should go to the dog pack. Curt gambled, in that clever-spouse way, that he would look good in my eyes and never have to deal with the dog.

I drove down the island and met Jon and Piki at the shelter. Piki was not an experienced car passenger and was, as always, terrified. Instead of riding in the back seat, as car-savvy dogs do, he sat or lay on the passenger-side front seat floor, between Jon's legs, panting and drooling with heat and anxiety. Piki didn't want to look out the window. He didn't want to sit up and see everything that was going on outside the car. He wanted to hide.

Also, it was Piki's first experience with the shadowy, cavernous light and unfamiliar clanking metallic sounds on the car deck of the ferry; the crowding of other cars; and people walking close beside the car. After we disembarked, there was the bright sunlight of the open, unforested land with no shadows, and the scary sounds of vehicles zipping past on the freeway.

We arrived at the obedience school at noon and were welcomed into Maureen's spacious office. Jon and I sat on a couch with Piki sitting on the floor between us.

Jon explained what he had to offer for Piki's future. Maureen nodded and asked several questions.

Since the real question was whether or not Piki could be trained, she then began to see what I knew about training.

"You and Piki, stand, please," Maureen said to me in a she-who-must-be-obeyed voice. Across the room there was a large airline kennel with its door open. "Put Piki into the crate," she told me.

If only she had asked for something else. Anything else! Piki had a fear of boxes, rectangles, doorways and anything else possibly resembling the trap in which we had tried for months to catch him. There was no way I'd be able to get him into the crate. I was going to have to explain immediately about his distrust of traps or any associated shape, or else make an ugly, failed spectacle of struggling, pushing and shoving to get him in.

Abruptly, I babbled about the trap we had tried to set for this dog and why he was so afraid of such small, enclosed spaces. I knew I was fumbling and was sure Maureen felt that as well.

She came out from behind her desk, walked over to me, took the leash from my hand, looked down at the dog, and crisply said, "Pikachu: kennel."

She led him to the airline kennel and stood to the side of the entrance, parallel to the open door. Piki furtively looked up at her. His eyes clearly registered that he knew she meant, *get in.*

It was dark in that kennel. And cramped. Would he test her to see if she really meant he was to willfully enter this dreaded place?

"Pikachu: kennel." A second time.

He went directly in.

Maureen bent over and swung the crate door shut, but instantly reopened it, and said, "Come."

Grateful, Piki bounded out.

Maureen then turned to me. "This is the key," she said. "You have to stand parallel to the direction you want the dog to go in. Not directly in front of him, which he perceives as blocking. Not behind him, which he sees as forcing."

I was impressed. I had taken two previous dogs to obedience schools, so I knew such schools existed to train the *owners* to train their dogs. But never had I seen a demonstration like this.

Maureen pressed a button on an intercom and a tall young man entered the office door. She handed him Piki's leash and the two of them disappeared down the hallway. Surprised, I didn't see any reluctance on Piki's part to go off with this stranger.

"He's going to work with Piki for a few minutes," Maureen explained. "He'll be able to judge the dog's ability and his willingness to learn."

While we waited, Maureen asked about Piki's background. I poured out the story about the original owner who kept his litter just until they were weaned, through Piki's adoption and escape, his abject fear of children and men, his living in the wild, his recapture, and his present comfort level at the shelter.

Jon and I asked Maureen about her training program, the costs involved, and whether it was feasible for either herself or her staff to train Piki.

There were, unfortunately, no openings at the school for some time, the fees were just about to go up, and—as Maureen pointed out—it would be a long commute to get Piki there.

My bubble of hope burst. I had seen that Maureen and her staff might work wonders with this dog.

"There are certainly other obedience teachers," Maureen said, "closer to your location and adequate."

The young man reappeared at the office door, and he and Maureen consulted briefly in the hallway. When she returned, she brought Pikachu to his place between Jon and me before going back to her desk. We sat motionless, waiting for her verdict.

"My colleague has found the dog to be smart and attentive," she said. "He is eager to learn."

She looked directly at me. "You take him." She paused. "And you train him."

She said that she could easily see that I loved Piki and was devoted to him from all that I had tried to do so far. I was in a state of shocked happiness.

Jon, of course, was not quite as invested in this decision as I had been. He held Piki in his lap all the way back to the shelter, comforting him on the difficult parts of the journey.

When we got off the ferry and started the drive inland from the dock, Piki could once again see the tall island trees and their shadows. Home. For the first time that day he relaxed and fell asleep.

XIII.
Over the Cliff

Late April 2001

A few days after I brought Pikichu home from the shelter, we returned from our late afternoon walk. I assumed Piki would come from the garage into the house along with Blue. But he didn't.

I had opened the car door, unhooked the leash from Piki's collar, let the dogs out and turned toward the door that led from the garage into the dining room. I opened it and Blue dashed in.

There was a moment of quiet.

No Piki.

With a groan I realized that I had not closed the overhead garage door to confine them before I let the dogs out of the car.

Was Piki in the garden? I went back outside to look.

I didn't see him anywhere. My heart began to drum.

I called, "Pikachu!" And repeated it again, to the wind, to the birds, to the trees.

It was just after rush hour from the Navy base on the road behind our house, but there was still quite a bit of traffic. I knew Piki was afraid of cars, but I didn't know if he actually knew how to keep from getting hit.

I ran around the house to look for him in our backyard.

No Piki.

I looked up and down the road. He could move fast, but I wasn't that far behind him. If I couldn't see him on the road, then he was probably in a neighbor's yard.

From where I was standing, I could see the yards across the road.

No Piki.

I crossed the road in order to get a better view of the yards on our side of the road.

Nothing.

Could he have crossed the road and kept going through the neighbor's back yard, over the cliff? Impossible. He wouldn't be that dumb. But then I was measuring his actions by my own standards of familiarity.

And my gut feeling was that I'd find Piki by the cliff. Hopefully, not as I had once found the body of an over-exuberant Irish Setter, dashed at the bottom.

I hate heights. I was filled with dread as I approached the edge of the sheer sandstone cliff. This cliff commands a view of the Strait of Juan de Fuca and Vancouver Island some forty miles away—and, more to the point, looks out over the beach almost three hundred feet below.

Careful not to get too close to the cliff's edge, I stopped on a vacant lot across from our house and peeked over.

There, below, I saw my new black dog, racing back and forth to the north and south ends of a six-foot wide, fifty-foot long grassy ledge located twenty to thirty feet below the top. Its boundaries were marked by eroding striations of orange and buff sandstone in every direction, mostly in sheer drops.

My heart plummeted. In the twenty years we had lived here, I had several times seen Navy Search and Rescue helicopters pluck unwary people off that cliff—drug users hiding out, lovers looking for privacy, kids seeking adventure and tempting fate. I had even seen dogs trapped on ledges, rescued by volunteer firemen roping up and going over the side after them.

Volunteer firemen! I rushed back home to phone.

"My dog has gone over the West Beach cliff and is trapped on a ledge about thirty feet below the top. Just five houses south of Fort Nugent on West Beach Road."

Then I raced back to the cliff to wait for the firemen and to keep watch on Piki. Heart pounding, I visualized the arrival of pickup trucks bearing burly young men carrying long coils of rope. They would tie one of the men into a cradle of rope and belay him over the side, as he clambered down, holding another rope for the dog....

That wasn't going to work. Piki would rather jump off his ledge and try to get away than allow himself to be approached by any strange man.

Maybe they would rope me up and let me go over?

But would a macho rescue team let a little old lady belay over a cliff? Not likely. For one thing, they'd never believe the little old lady might have some experience with this kind of maneuver—and even I had to admit, said experience had been a long time ago.

I ran home, dialed 911, and cancelled the previous emergency call. Fortunately, the personnel had not yet been dispatched.

Grabbing a leash, I sprinted back to the cliff. Piki had stopped his frantic running and was standing still, panting heavily, tongue lolling, the rolling whites of his eyes showing desperation. He seemed to have finally realized that he was in dire trouble.

"Piki," I called to him. He looked up at me. I tried to speak softly and calmly and get him to focus on me so he would overcome his panic. Meanwhile, I walked back and forth across the top of the cliff, searching for a place where the slope was less steep, where I might be able to guide him back under his own power, or where I might be able to go down a little to show him the way and encourage him. I understood that he must have gone down in progressive jumps. If he had sailed out over the cliff in a single leap, his momentum would have taken him a lot farther down.

"It's okay," I said to him. "Just stay where you are. Don't panic. And, for God's sake, don't go any farther down." I struggled to keep my voice sounding calm and confident and to maintain the connection between us.

I found soft, loose sand just below the top of the cliff. It was behind the house to the north from where Pikachu was trapped. The loose sand only went about ten feet down and, once dislodged, it started to slide, but at least I could get a foothold. If I could keep my balance and lean into the cliff, I shouldn't slide too far down with the sand.

From that point, there were several other soft spots on the slope that led south toward Pikachu's ledge. Between them were expanses of sheer rock, where footholds seemed impossible, but these were narrow enough that Piki could jump over them to the next soft landing place. If he would. If only he would pay attention to me as I guided him, he might be able to make it toward me on his own.

There were few handholds as I sat on the edge and eased over the side, teetering as the sand began to give way. Normally, I would have been terrified, but my attention was focused on my baby, and I now understood that only I could deal with him.

I wasn't sure Piki recognized the command *come*, but when I said it, he looked up and we made eye contact. He must have judged me as being closer than before, being within reach. He bolted over the rock, through the sand, and into my arms so forcefully that I almost fell and carried us both to the bottom.

But I didn't fall. I had Piki. And I held him tight.

Both of us were panting from fear, excitement, and relief. I hooked the leash into his collar. We held our place together for a minute to compose ourselves for the final ten-foot climb. Then we turned to face it.

I knew it would be easier for Piki than for me. He could spring up the slope in one jump, while the sand would slip out backward from underneath my churning feet. But his leash was only six-feet long and I didn't want to drag him back. There was no way I was going to let go of that leash, either, or he would be gone again at the top.

And then there was no more time to think: Piki jumped. He bounded up, the leash snapped taught, straining—and Piki pulled me to the top.

In shock and disbelief, I crawled a few feet away from the cliff's edge. The two of us sat, pressed close together, catching our breaths—physically and emotionally spent.

Then we stood and went home, Piki walking meekly beside me.

Part Three

Becoming a Full - Time Mom

XIV.

A Whole New World

After our evaluation by the head of the obedience school, Piki came home from the animal shelter with me on a foster-care basis. It meant my giving up volunteering at the shelter and becoming a full-time mother for him.

I had to walk a delicate line between dealing with this dog and the other males in my life—Curt and Blue—so I didn't commit immediately to adopting Piki.

For me, keeping a pet is like being married to it: until death do us part. My husband feels that way, too, although in this case I soon began to hear, "How long is this going to last?" And "When will he stay in the same room with me?"

I felt sorry for Curt. Whenever he walked into the bedroom or family room, Piki would stand and leave. Curt tried to be friendly and cheerful, make direct eye contact, reach out to the dog. What Curt didn't understand was that Piki perceived direct eye contact and reaching out to him as a threat. Piki's eyes began to express fear whenever he saw Curt coming toward him. The dog would rise to his feet and slink out of the room—utterly rejecting my husband.

Curt and I had the best of intentions without the know-how to carry them out. For us it was strictly on-the-job training. Trial and error.

Late one day when we were both particularly tired, Curt accosted me in the kitchen. "I won't put up with this any longer," he said. "It's him or me."

The melodrama could have been amusing, but in my fatigue my first reaction was anger. I was acting from my most noble intentions to redeem the lost. I was working my buns off with this dog, attending to everyone else in the family, and doing whatever else that needed to be done. I was doing ten times the work Curt was doing, and he was the one who was whimpering. You go, I thought. I'll keep Piki!

Of course, I didn't say aloud what I was thinking. I turned my back to Curt, held on to the edge of the sink, gritted my teeth, and somehow kept the replies that were forming inside me from being said aloud. When I didn't acknowledge his challenge after a few moments, Curt walked away.

Once he'd left, I took a calming breath and tried to put myself in his place. How would I react if my spouse had brought home cats and dogs that desperately needed help and some of them—as I had with Sweetie—without any advance notice? Almost all of these animals were all right in the end, but that took time, and working with them upset the calm routine of our life. It certainly was not always comfortable. I had anticipated the major scope of Piki's problems, but Curt had not. Now that the reality of these problems was manifesting in our home, Curt was overwhelmed and under-appreciated—by both me and Piki. I could certainly understand that.

And Piki's problems were many: the dog wasn't housebroken and he had not the slightest concept of right or wrong behavior, loyalty, respect, or even any special friendliness toward humans, especially toward children and men. A day never passed without tears: Piki's or mine. Or both. I really didn't know if this was going to work.

Curt's ultimatum, partly motivated by the discomfort he imagined that Blue was also feeling, was impossible for me to ignore. Knowing Curt, I realized that he meant that I had limited time with this dog, that he wouldn't live with the situation forever. But I had no idea how long this process was going to take. I was operating by intuition with Pikachu. I was learning from my mistakes. Deadlines and demands were the last things we needed. I wanted to keep Piki.

On the other hand, I had a great husband. I loved him. I wanted to keep him, too.

Following Maureen's example, I began by trying to crate-train Piki. Pet owners who train their puppy that its airline kennel is its home, its comfort, its refuge, swear that the animal would rather curl up there than be almost any other place. It's a doggie security blanket.

Sounded good. My rationale was that Piki would have a haven where he would be out of the hubbub, where he'd feel safe and quiet. Having his own special place was also an answer to possible territorial issues with Blue, who, after all, had seniority and wasn't likely to willingly yield it. Furthermore, an animal doesn't usually foul its own nest, so it could be expected that the as-yet-to-be-housebroken Pikachu would not pee or poop inside his crate.

Now, where to place the crate so that Piki could be on the fringe of activity when he needed to be and still not feel isolated and excluded? For starters, I chose the guest bedroom.

I made space there for our large airline crate. I fixed a piece of sturdy cardboard on the bottom inside to provide a level floor and placed a soft blanket toward the rear with food and water bowls near the front door. The door was open-wire, and the kennel's top had small wire windows.

It looked so good to me, I was ready to crawl in myself.

I found Piki, snapped a leash onto his collar and walked him into the guest bedroom, closing the door behind us. Asking the dog to sit, I removed the leash, stood tall and to the side of the kennel door, parallel to the path I wanted Piki to take to enter the kennel. I looked him in the eye and firmly said, "Piki, kennel." I was trying to channel Maureen.

The dog started to back up, squirm away. What had worked for Maureen at the Northwest Academy of Canine Training clearly wasn't working for me here.

I squatted down, grabbed Piki, and shoved him through the kennel door, shutting the door quickly behind him. Then I handed in doggie treats through the wires of the door, hoping to distract Piki from his discomfort. As he always did when he was unhappy, he rejected them.

I stood up, sweating.

There were two major problems to crate training Piki. One, he wasn't a puppy. Two, in its size and configuration, the kennel was almost identical to the failed humane trap that Piki had learned to so distrust.

I was, however, committed to making an attempt at the crate training. I left the room, feeling like the mother of a young child having a temper tantrum—should I hold him and comfort him or let him cry himself to sleep?

Piki made a herding-dog whine. Continuously. For the next hour. He seemed to be saying, *I know this isn't right.*

I finally let him out of his crate because it was time for our late afternoon walk, to be followed by dinner when we returned.

After dinner, it was back into the kennel. Not with a joyous, confident, "Piki: Kennel," but once again with a physical struggle that seemed brutal even to me—it must have for sure to him.

As I've mentioned, Piki wasn't housebroken, something we learned in the only way one can learn such a thing: the hard way. The wet way.

Piki had two modes for peeing inside the house: the fear-motivated fast leak and the gusher. The gusher was what a normal dog who had to relieve himself would do outside, except that Piki didn't yet know he was supposed to do it outside. The fear-pee was when Curt, or any other man, looked his way and made eye contact. Piki then trembled uncontrollably and yellow drops of urine seeped forth.

One day a friend named Ted, a reputed dog-lover, stopped by the house. He and Curt were talking in the kitchen, when Piki made a wrong turn and wandered in.

"So, this is your new dog," Ted boomed. "Looks like a dog pound special."

Ted looked at Piki directly. The dog froze and tucked his tail between his legs—a sign of fear—until it almost reached his chin. Almost immediately, Piki started trembling, shaking, and leaking. A little yellow puddle formed on the vinyl floor.

"What the hell did you get, a fraidy cat? What a wimp! Doesn't he know he's supposed to take a leak outside? He's pissing all over the floor!"

Piki hustled away, dribbling as he went. I hurriedly tried to mop up as Ted stood there, mocking my baby. I started to explain that Piki was a wild dog, that we had just brought him home, that he was terrified of men, that he wasn't yet housebroken, that he would take time and patience.

Ted brushed off my explanations with a laugh. "Wait till I tell Jim your new dog pissed all over the kitchen."

I felt a sinking in the pit of my stomach. This was how it would be: people would think I was crazy to put up with Piki; Curt's friends would shame him.

Even though I despaired of the spectacle Piki was making, I felt protective of my baby, and I could have cheerfully murdered Ted. What kind of friend was this? A Guardian of the Conventional? A Keeper of Cleanliness? Whatever had happened to compassion?

After seeing Ted out to his car, my husband returned to help me finish cleaning up.

Curt was fuming—but not in the way I had expected. "Fine friend he turned out to be! He never even tried to understand. Now the jerk will tell all our other friends that Piki peed in front of him on the kitchen floor. Big dog-lover he is."

I don't know if Curt even realized that he was defending Piki. I kissed him, and he got a wondering expression on his face. He may not have realized it, but in that moment, he signed up. Curt and I would be taking on the insensitive world together. I was already making silent plans.

For one thing, I tried to anticipate when Piki had to pee. When he got up in the morning, certainly; after breakfast and dinner; before bedtime. I couldn't let him loose in the yard because he would surely run away, so each time I had to drop what I was doing, put him on a leash and take him out.

I was, however, utterly helpless in the face of this dog's natural needs. I remember vividly one afternoon when I started to take him out. I put on his leash, and headed toward the door. I felt him lag behind me and turned to see why. Piki was standing in the family room agonizingly close to the deck door, hind legs slightly bent, Niagara Falls gushing out into an enormous yellow puddle that slowly seeped into the dark teal carpet.

Curt and I liked to entertain friends in our home, but that was unthinkable under these circumstances. Even though we had the carpet professionally cleaned many times, the urine had soaked into the pad. As soon as the afternoon sun was shining through the floor-to-ceiling windows in our west-facing living room, the not-so-delicate fragrance of ammonia would rise from the carpet and fill the room. We opened wide the windows and deck doors, we turned on the ceiling fan, but none of it worked to get rid of that pungent smell.

It was even trickier to anticipate when Piki might have to go out during the night. Yes, he stayed in his crate at night, but for Piki the crate did not mean security; it meant confinement. Piki made it abundantly clear that he did not consider this cage to be his own little nest.

I was already feeding Piki in Curt's den, so that there would be no territorial issues over food between Piki and Blue. Now I moved the whole crate into the den, the supposed advantage being that it was closer to the master bedroom and we'd use the crate chiefly at night so that Piki couldn't roam the house at will while we were sleeping. (He had by now shredded a third shoe of mine, all coming, of course, from separate pairs.) Theoretically, Piki would feel more a part of the family when we bedded down—Curt, me, Blue, and the three cats (Tessa, Halo, and Puck), all of whom slept in the same bedroom. Piki would be able to watch his buddy, Blue, from the den as Blue slept on his mat at the foot of our bed.

Invariably, at some hour of the night, Piki would begin to cry and whine—his sign to me that he needed to go outside. I'd throw a white bathrobe over my pajamas and a navy blue parka over that, put on a knit cap and gloves, hook up the leash, and out we'd go.

Sometimes we just wandered around our backyard, stepping carefully in the dark to avoid "land mines"—leavings from other visits Piki and Blue had made to the yard. Sometimes, I'd attach Piki's twenty-foot leash, and we'd walk down the road of our little cul-de-sac neighborhood.

Almost invariably if we walked on our road, at some point the 4 a.m. stillness would be shattered by the bass vibrations of a rapper. The first time it happened, I feared for my safety—here I was, a defenseless woman walking the streets in her bathrobe—and I tried to hide myself and my outlandish ensemble behind a tree. But it proved to be the teenage son of a family down the street, driving home from his night job stocking grocery store shelves. He waved a cheery hello to me, his white-toothed smile gleaming in the dark. Each time this happened, there would be a few other dark, silent cars parked near this boy's house, and the kids would quietly exit their cars to join my neighbor as he went inside, all of them smiling hellos to me. After that family moved away, I learned that those cheery young men were the neighborhood drug dealer and his customers.

If I hadn't been walking Piki in the dead of the night, I would never have known.

XV.

Housebreaking

Summer 2001

Blue, Piki's canine mentor, eventually taught Piki not to pee in the house. And this is the reason why —Blue was an absolute sweetheart, but he had one major problem: he compulsively drank over a gallon of water a day. Consequently, he had to go outside to pee, *often*. Blue would signal me by standing at the deck door, dancing up and down, while I rushed to let him out into the backyard.

None of the vets we took him to was able to explain or solve Blue's drinking problem, but I think it was due to the extreme stress of the months of neglect he had endured.

Before Blue went to the WAIF shelter, he had been the resident pet dog at an adult family nursing home. There, he had witnessed his beloved owner—the owner of the home—slowly die of cancer early in 1999. After her death, an unauthorized employee kept the home open. At the time, no one knew that this employee was addicted to drugs and was neglecting the patients. State authorities eventually removed the patients and shut down the home, but this squatter remained in it —still unauthorized by the late owner's family—along with Blue. Soon, the power and water utilities cut off service. In December, the bank foreclosed on the home and, together with an animal control officer, bankers stepped into plastic trash bags and pulled them up their legs before they entered the house.

Inside they found Blue, alone in a closed room, matted with feces, his claws so long that they curled under. He could barely walk. He had apparently been fed regularly, but never let out. Because it was doubtful that he was still housebroken, the person Blue's late owner had designated to take him reneged, and the dog went instead to the animal shelter.

That's where I found him a couple days before New Year's Eve, 1999. I didn't want to start the new century and millennium without a dog. Our beloved Nacho had died in 1998. At the time Curt had said, "No more dogs. It's just too hard to lose them." We had gone for a whole year with just our cats.

In the face, Blue resembled Nacho. When I took Curt to the shelter to ask if he approved my choice, Blue had the good sense to rest his head on Curt's knee. That sealed the deal. We took a chance on Blue's remembering to pee outdoors, and he did do that. It's just that we'd had no idea how often that would be.

When we brought Blue home from the shelter, I made an internal promise to the dog that I would do whatever it took to keep him. He was just about to turn eight, and, as it turned out, he still had good control of his bladder. Early on, I averaged getting up to let him out only about three times during the course of a night. By the time he was old and infirm, it would be as many as eight.

Although I couldn't just let Piki run loose to do his business in the yard, as Blue could, I did snap a leash on Piki and go out at the same time I let Blue out. When Blue peed, I soothingly cooed, in a saccharin voice intended mainly for Piki to hear, "Good dog, Blue. Good pee." Then, as soon as Piki began to pee, I used my best praise-voice to coax him to associate *good* with desired behavior and *pee* with the action performed.

Piki soon caught on. Besides, whenever he had an accident in the house, he also caught the look of disgust on Blue's face.

There was another clincher in the housebreaking process. Early in Piki's life with us, we had boarded both dogs at a local kennel while we were away on short trips.

Blue had spent most of his life inside a house and clearly loathed the damp, gray, wire-fenced kennel setting. For Piki, it was Home Sweet Home. The chain-link fencing, the bare cement floors wet from being hosed clean rang for him the sweet chimes of familiarity.

The daily routine at the kennel allowed a short time for the dogs to be individually released from their pens to the exercise yard when the employees reported for work in the morning. It was assumed the dogs would take advantage of this time to relieve themselves. Then they were expected to happily return to their kennels.

When we made the arrangements to board him, I explained to staff that Piki might not understand that this was his time to pee and that I wasn't at all sure he would come when they called him. They took him anyhow.

Piki and Blue roomed together in the same kennel, which meant they would be fed at the same time, let outside together, and brought back inside at the same time.

Although Piki didn't pee outside the first morning, it soon became clear to him that he'd better take advantage of the opportunity at the next exercise period. He also observed that, when called, Blue loped back to the kennel to eat breakfast. Piki galloped after him— something that eventually helped Piki to begin to better understand the *come* command, as well.

XVI.

Running Free

Now that I had become a full-time mother, I remembered my own mother saying that youngsters napped on time and slept through the night when they were played out. I encouraged Piki to use his boundless energy to exercise as much as possible, hoping he would be too worn out to make mischief during the day and would sleep serenely through the night.

More than anything else, Piki loved to run. I had to find a way to allow him to run and still have him return to me. We had a fairly big backyard, but it wasn't big enough for him to really sprint. Moreover, we didn't want to diminish our view of the ocean and Vancouver Island by fencing it.

Not all dog owners are as fortunate as we are to have a place or an opportunity for their pets to run off-lead, albeit closely watched. Some less-than-responsible owners allow their dogs to run loose in their neighborhoods and on public lands. These dogs, untrained and unsupervised, often create havoc. Some dogs have a dangerous prey drive—a compulsion to hunt—and should not, cannot, be allowed uncontrolled freedom.

Just one look at a large dog can make many people feel threatened, and there is a real potential of threat to other animals if a large dog is uncontrolled. But the issue, I think, is that of defining *control*.

A dog can be controlled within a fence or by the limits of a leash, but better yet, it can be controlled through its bond to a human master. Such a bond means that the master and dog are "on the same page" and know one another's expectations and limitations. Our culture promotes the inherent premise of man's *dominion* over animals. This gives humanity license to treat or mistreat animals as we please. More and more, people are beginning to recognize the value of animals as *partners* to humanity. It is this relationship that I wanted to achieve with Piki and that I was seeking through a necessarily fumbling process of trial and error.

I often took Piki and Blue to a deserted nearby beach at low tide for our walks. I chose this place because when the day came that I did let Piki off-lead to run freely, he could escape from me in only two directions rather than four. The beach was bound to the east by a high cliff and to the west by the ocean. If Piki got away from me, he would have to run north to get past me and Blue in order to return to the road and the car—not really all that difficult, but we might provide a brief deterrent. If he ran south on the beach—oh, mama!—Piki could go forever and what a long walk it would be to follow him!

In the Pacific Northwest the tides are characteristically low during daylight hours from March through October. In this summer of 2001, we could enjoy miles of isolated beaches, limited only by the amount of time and physical exertion we wanted to spend.

I began by dutifully walking Piki on a twenty-foot lead, but I soon found that was as boring for me as it was for Piki. He wanted to go where Blue went, smell what Blue smelled. I scrambled to keep up with them. This was Piki's teenage summer and he was particularly energetic at the start of each walk; I was sixty-two years old, and, although I had always been active, I wasn't going to be able to keep up with him for very long.

One day, I got the bright idea to make a slipknot out of the long leash, pull it over my head, and fix it around my waist. In theory, I could slow Piki down by leaning backwards, and I didn't have to hold the leash constantly with one or both hands. This worked well—for a while.

When we were walking on the beach one afternoon in this manner, Piki spotted his first flock of wading birds scurrying along at the edge of waves surging onshore. Like a shot, he accelerated toward them, jerking the long leash tight, then tighter, around my waist as it pulled me forward. Instead of slowing Piki down, the leash almost tore me in half. I couldn't breathe, and I felt such a sharp jab of pain that I was afraid I had suffered lasting lower-back damage. I immediately abandoned that not-too-clever idea.

I weighed the pros and cons of unhooking the leash altogether: I couldn't expect Piki to come directly back to me, but Blue would come when I called, and Piki might do as Blue did. It would probably take a longer time for Piki to come, but then, I had a couple hours free on this particular afternoon.

I unhooked the leash from his collar.

It took several seconds before Piki realized that he was free. His expression showed disbelief—and then, sheer JOY.

He tore down the beach full-tilt about two hundred yards, then turned and ran back toward me at top speed, grinning as he swept past me. Next, he turned toward the slides of loose sand that poured to the foot of the eroding cliffs. He loved running across these wide sand-slide deltas, deep and soft and tough going, but to him exhilarating. Then he raced straight up to the top of the sand-slides, thirty and forty feet high, paused at the apex, turned to face the bottom, sat and slid all the way down on his rear end.

When he seemed to tire from playing on the sand-slides, I threw sticks into the water for him. I tossed sticks for Blue to retrieve, too, but Blue was not a water dog. He was happy to fetch his stick, lie down on the wet sand for a while and gnaw on it. Piki, however, must have inherited some genes from a good Lab parent, because he braved breaking waves to swim out and retrieve his sticks. When he emerged from the shallows, he was wreathed in rainbows, shaking water out of his coat. He dropped his stick on the shore and then charged back to the sand deltas to collect a full load of sand clinging to his wet hair.

After a while this heavy baggage of sand began to weigh Piki down, and his frantic energy ebbed. Now I had to plot how I would catch him so we could all go home.

If Blue and I turned to go toward the car, Piki probably would follow. It was important, however, to get him on a leash before we reached the parking area. If he got away from me in the parking lot, it was doubtful I could ever catch him, and he wouldn't be able to find his own way home because we always went to the beach by car.

I called Blue, and he ran to me. Piki followed him and came near me, but not quite close enough for me to grab his collar. Coy, he danced just out of reach until we were within sight of the car. I didn't dare go closer to the car without him on a leash, so I backtracked a few hundred yards and sat on a driftwood log. I lured Blue over to me with the treats I carried in my pocket. Piki came up to the log and nuzzled my fist that hid a treat for him. When I moved my hand to my lap, he persisted, coming close enough for me to snag his collar with my other hand.

That's what happened the first time I let Piki off lead. Each successive time we did this, he became more savvy.

I was not a total stranger to this process. In the years before we moved to Washington state, my husband and I had endured it with one of our cats almost every time we stayed at our cabin in Alaska during the summer. Spooky liked nothing better than to spend the whole time—night and day—under the cabin hunting shrews, tiny animals resembling mice. When we packed up to leave for home, the ordeal of catching her would begin.

Once, I managed to get Spooky out by sweeping a long-handled broom horizontally on the ground, forcing her toward me and then grabbing her. On our next visit, however, she was broom-savvy, and that ploy no longer worked. Another time Spooky condescended to an offer of food; afterward, never again. One by one, she learned our strategies and then outwitted them.

The only thing that ever worked twice was her fascination with my husband's electric razor. I had spent a half-hour kneeling next to the cabin, coaxing her to come close with no success. After a few days of growing a beard, Curt decided to shave before we returned to the city. While the razor was running, he came outside to see if I was making any progress. Well, I hadn't been, until then. But Spooky became curious at the sound of the razor, and all-innocence, appeared at the edge of the cabin. I bagged her immediately, and we left for home in record time. She was such a sucker for the sound of the razor that she actually fell for it one more time.

Knowing from this experience that Piki would become increasingly more devious about returning to me, I only rarely let him off-lead at the beach. But each time I did, I could feel the burst of exhilaration that he experienced in being free. I did it a few more times that summer, choosing afternoons when I would have several hours to retrieve him.

It always seemed like a good idea in the moment I was unhooking the leash from his collar and he was dashing away in delight. Two to three hours later, when I still hadn't caught him, I didn't appreciate the gamesmanship quite so much. I longed for the day when I could let Piki run free and then choose to willingly return to me.

Playing dead is a famous old trick for dogs. In my increasing frustration at getting Piki to come to me, I finally seized upon the idea of *my* playing dead. Only when I was certain he was watching me from the distance, *I* was the body crumpling to the sand and lying there, inert.

Just before I dropped, lifeless, I glanced to make sure I wasn't going down on sand-covered rocks and that the leash hook was readily handy.

It took time.

Blue, attentive as ever, trotted up to nuzzle me. Even if I was in a position where I couldn't peek at the dog to see which one it was, I could tell it was Blue because he was more concerned about my welfare and likely to come first. He also had long guard hairs that hung down and touched my face or arm when he sniffed me.

If I lay there for more minutes on end without moving, Piki would eventually come close. He warily sniffed my hair, then nudged me with his snout. I had to stifle laughter as he worked to revive me, licking my arms, neck, and face. When he was finally in a position where I could grab him, I miraculously sprang back to life and hooked him up.

I brushed sand out of my hair and clothes as we walked back to the car, our game for that day at an end.

XVII.

Black Devil Dog from Hell

August 3-6, 2001

One Saturday we had returned from our late afternoon walk and the dogs had finished eating when, out of the corner of my eye, I noticed Piki crossing through the living room on his way to lie down in the family room. He was close to the deck door when he saw me glance up and followed my eyes to the door, which was cracked open a couple inches for the cats to come and go. I immediately moved to close it, but Piki moved faster.

Helpless, I watched him duck out, his skinny black torso squeezing through, pushing the door open wider.

Gone. By the time I got to the door, seconds later, I couldn't see him. I could have kicked myself.

Was he over the cliff again?

I rushed outside to look.

Nothing. If he went over the cliff this time, he went all the way down.

I ran back to tell Curt that Piki had gotten out the door, that I didn't know where he was, and that I would be walking the beach to the bottom of the cliff opposite our house.

I drove to the closest place where I could park at sea level, a little over a mile away. I parked and started walking south. The dogs and I regularly walked on this beach, but that was at low tide when the beach was wide and welcoming. Right now the tide was high, and the walking area—close to the bottom of the cliff—was narrow and rocky.

The salmon were starting to run, and I passed a fisherman casting his line from the beach.

"Have you seen a black dog running alone?"

He hadn't.

As fast as I could, I ran and walked the mile that brought me to the beach below our house, straining all the while to see any new black form I might spot on the slope above me. Since a big bulge in the rock near the bottom of the cliff made it impossible to see up the slope from directly beneath, it was easier to scan from a distance. A distinctive Douglas Fir tree, whose wind-sculpted branches faced away from the water, grew just halfway down the cliff from the empty lot across the street from our house, so I knew exactly where I was.

No black body at the bottom. That was good news.

Could Piki be hung up somewhere on the slope in a spot I couldn't see? Or had he learned his lesson last time and chosen not to go to the cliff at all?

There was a cloudbank on the west horizon. The sun sank early, and my spirits sank with it. The wind off the water was getting chillier. I walked back to the car and drove in the direction of home, cruising the closest main roads, searching the yards of the houses. Then I drove up and down the side streets, doing the same.

No Pikachu.

The sky was getting dark.

Would he come back home? Should I sleep by the deck door that night in case he did? If he didn't come back, where would he spend the night? My intuition told me that if Piki wasn't on the cliff, then he'd headed for the woods. Perhaps the woods southeast of our house? Or had he gone to the deep woods that bordered the big meadow to the north and east of the house?

My best guess was northeast. That was the direction from which I sometimes heard coyotes howling in the night. I shuddered with that empty, sick feeling known only by someone who has ever had a missing loved one.

It was the end of a long day and I was tired and hungry. Now it would be a long night of putting together lost-dog posters that I could distribute the next morning.

I made myself a sandwich and took it into my computer room. Soon, I found a photo that would work for the poster. It showed Piki's whole body and his long, thin, Greyhound-like muzzle.

I slept on the couch in the living room with only the screen door closed, but Piki didn't appear that night.

The next morning I set out with the copies of my poster encased in clear plastic sleeves, a hammer, and a bunch of nails. I headed away from the beach to the main east-west road between West Beach and Oak Harbor.

I knew enough not to look for Piki where there would be many people, but I needed a lead—any information from someone who might have seen him.

I met a friendly workman at the second intersection, where I was getting ready to put up a poster. Showing him the poster I asked if he had seen this dog.

I was shocked when he said, "Yes, I think so." Then he asked, "Is he wearing a red bandana along with his collar?"

That had to be Pikachu; I had put on that bandana just for fun the day before. "When did you see him?"

"Just before dark last night, when I had to call it quits with my work here."

"Did you notice which way he headed?"

"He went north from here, on Zylstra." The man pointed in the direction of the cross street, which dead-ended just a few blocks farther north in farmland bordering on the extensive woods I had thought Piki might have gone to.

I thanked him and tacked my poster onto a prominent pole. Now I knew what direction I would head in next: to the northeast, to the woods.

I drove to Even Down, a little community off West Beach Road, which bordered on the woods. I stopped to see friends I knew there so I could find out from them the best way to walk farther into the trees. They described a trail I could take into the woods. After putting up a few more posters in the neighborhood, I parked as near as I could to the trail.

I could see that these woods were ideal for Piki. The trees extended at least a mile from west to east and almost a mile from south to north—just like his old home on Central Whidbey.

I followed the trail east for quite a while. Then, I stopped, seeing a teenage boy in a small clearing ahead of me. He looked strange, somehow disoriented, and I was instantly afraid of him. But he had seen me, too, and I felt that if he really were dangerous, it might provoke him if I turned or backed away. He was alone, so I approached him with my poster and asked if he'd seen the dog.

"Yeah. Maybe."

"When did you see him?"

"A couple hours ago."

"Was it right around here?"

"Yeah."

"Was he wearing a red bandana around his neck?"

"No. I didn't see nuthin' but a collar."

I was so hoping he had really seen Piki, but the no-bandana part left me unsure. And from his uncommunicative manner, I didn't know if I could believe any of what this young man had said.

My trek took me to the edge of the farmland where Zylstra Road dead-ended. I squeezed through the barbed wire fence and walked along the meadow, where it was easier to walk. I whistled and called for Piki. No response. Another hour passed, and I went back to my car.

By now I had a better sense of the extent of the woods. If I crossed to the far northern edge, I'd be in the valley near Swantown Lake. Beautiful dairy farmland bordered the lake, and this extended to a golf course at the east end. Piki could make his way from one small community of houses to another through the trees.

I drove to the Swantown Lake area, where I met a young man working in his fields. I recognized him as a vegetable vendor at the local farmers' markets. He listened with interest as I described my lost-dog problem. He said he'd keep his eyes open for Piki and let me know if he saw him. I left him a copy of my poster with my phone number.

Hours had passed. It was now late afternoon. I returned home to walk Blue and report to my husband that I was still alive, that I had a lead on Piki's whereabouts, but no success just yet.

After dinner and a brief rest, I set out again in the car, driving as close as I could to the woods, calling, "Piki, Piki."

Nothing.

Night fell again. I slept next to the deck door for a second night, hoping Piki would find his way home, worrying about him going more than twenty-four hours now without food. Here we were again, repeating the ordeal of his wandering at large on Central Whidbey. Where was he finding water and a safe place to sleep? I assumed that I was the only person he would willingly come to. Could he actually have been taken in by someone else? All these questions pulsed through my exhausted brain.

I would just have to start looking all over again the next day.

On Monday I repeated much of what I had done the day before, with no more to show for my efforts. No one I met had seen Piki. Just before dark, a little after 8:30, I popped Blue into the car and we drove our circuit one more time.

In the big, open field northeast of our house, I saw a small figure moving, close to the dark mass of trees. Was it a dog?

The light was dim and the figure was far away, but it seemed to be coming out of the woods and toward us.

I parked and sat inside the car, rolling down the windows on the right side to get a better view for both Blue and myself. I watched Blue's body language. He was alert, focused on the dog.

Yes. It was a dog. Dark-colored, medium-sized, head and tail down, moving slowly, with little energy, coming our way.

I jumped out of the car and opened the rear door to release Blue. Piki had come to Blue in the wild. Maybe he would come to him now.

Blue and I climbed down the roadside bank and approached the dog. He was now close enough to us to identify. It was Pikachu. Tired, dirty, hungry for sure. His red bandana rolled so thin around his neck and so dirty, it was hard to tell he had it on.

After two days and two nights, was he on his way back home? We'll never know.

He ran to Blue, shying away from me, wild again. But when I called Blue to head back to the car, Piki came along, and I grabbed his collar.

I sighed with relief but no great happiness, and the three of us got back into the car and went home.

Now that the crisis was resolved, a black wave of negative feelings welled up in me—thoughts of all the wasted time, worry, and effort of the past couple days. I knew I had left the deck door open and that my body language let Piki know about that open door. But in this moment, I blamed him.

As he passed me entering the house, I snarled, "Black devil dog from hell! Get your buns into the house. And stay there!"

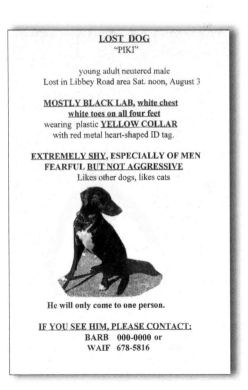

LOST DOG
"PIKI"

young adult neutered male
Lost in Libbey Road area Sat. noon, August 3

MOSTLY BLACK LAB, white chest
white toes on all four feet
wearing plastic **YELLOW COLLAR**
with red metal heart-shaped ID tag.

EXTREMELY SHY, ESPECIALLY OF MEN
FEARFUL BUT NOT AGGRESSIVE
Likes other dogs, likes cats

He will only come to one person.

IF YOU SEE HIM, PLEASE CONTACT:
BARB   000-0000 or
WAIF   678-5816

XVIII.
Starting Obedience School

Mid August 2001

The time had come to find a local obedience school. An acquaintance from the animal shelter, Mary, was offering a beginners' class that started within a few weeks. The timing was right and I signed up for it.

I had been to obedience schools with two previous dogs, and both dogs had learned to perform well off-lead, but neither of those schools was available anymore. I knew from those classes that the object of any obedience school is to teach the pet owner how to train his own dog. The big advantage of doing it in a class, rather than just at home, is the interaction among the dogs—both desirable and also, for training purposes, undesirable. At least everyone could learn what to do and not do to solve an altercation between dogs.

The first big lesson in my previous classes was in the proper use of choke chains. Many people use them improperly and actually choke their dogs. Some regard the metal links in the chain as brutal and substitute a braided fabric slip-collar, but, if properly used, the *sound* of the metal links is what a dog in training learns to listen for and respond to, as well as the brief pressure on the dog's neck. Second, and equally important to proper use of the chain, is an immediate voice reward for a dog's good behavior:

good dog, good job, good heel, and so forth in an enthusiastic and loving voice, followed quickly by a gentle touch.

Mary's advertising announced, in large letters: No Choke Chains. I knew that choke chains worked well, but I thought this trainer must have another technique to offer and that I would be learning something new, which is always useful.

The classes were held at a building located in the forests of Central Whidbey in a different area from Piki's woodsy stamping grounds. Mercifully, the building was covered and enclosed and all Piki's classes were inside. From the moment I put on his leash, let him out of the car, and led him into the building, he was looking around at the trees, clearly checking any possibility of escape into the woods.

The teacher had instructed us to bring to class a plastic bag filled with small dog treats. They were to serve to motivate and reward the dogs. No old-fashioned corrections with choke chains—just pop a treat in the dog's mouth when he did the right thing. Neither did this teacher encourage the gentle touches and loving words in an oily, oozing voice. Food was motivation and reward.

Most dogs are food oriented, so I have no doubt that this approach was successful with many of Mary's young protégés. Piki, however, had been offered food as bait in a trap, and so he viewed offered food with suspicion and rejected the whole concept of working for treats. The only time Piki ever accepted a treat was when he was totally relaxed, comfortable, and unstressed. This was not going to be the case in these classes.

Mary's first session was unlike anything I had ever before experienced. By whatever means possible, I had to get Piki to sit or lie down. Then I was to stand over him and gradually lower my body until I was virtually sitting on his back, though without putting my weight on him. This, the teacher explained, would demonstrate to the dog that the human was alpha and in control.

She never mentioned the dominance games that dogs always play when they meet each other for the first time. It is crucial to each dog to find out which one is dominant, what is the pecking order. Their circling, stiff-legged stances, their postures are all part of the show. If a male dog succeeds in mounting another male, it has nothing to do with sex—as humans usually think—but, rather, with showing which is the top dog, the dominant dog.

Most of these owners had never attended any other obedience classes before, and they had little or no knowledge of what this dominant action represented to the dog. Furthermore, their dogs were mostly six months to a year old and in the submissive baby-stage. In contrast, Piki was a young adult, just a few months short of two years. He fully realized that he was, symbolically, getting screwed. A male dog. By a human female. He was not happy about it.

When dogs voluntarily submit to domination, canine or human, they roll over on their backs, belly-up. It is a sign of surrender in which they offer their unprotected throats to their dominator. Piki had never yet bellied up for me. When he let me pet him on the day I caught him, he craved just to be touched. He hadn't voluntarily traded his freedom for comfort and security. Now he was being forced to acknowledge human dominance. He glowered at me indignantly.

The next step was for the dog to learn the command *watch me*. I was told to walk Piki straight ahead a short distance on a standard six-foot lead, and then tell him, "Watch me," as we turned to change direction. If he made eye contact with me to anticipate the turn, I was to instantly reward him with a treat. The object was to get the dog to watch its master in order to anticipate stops, starts, and changes of speed and direction.

Good in theory. Good for semi-civilized dogs with a desire to please their owners.

Piki bolted into the lead, dragging me along without paying the slightest attention to me or my repeated *watch me* commands until I dug in my heels, and he screeched to a halt, strangling on a normal collar at the end of a taut leash. His eyes bulging, he looked back at me as I tried to shove a scorned treat into his mouth.

He spit it out.

We went weekly, and Piki repeated the same basic reaction as we worked through *heel, sit, down, stay, come.* He eyed the building's exits at every turn, obviously aching to get out of there. One thing he learned: if he never did anything right, at least he wouldn't get food shoved at him.

About this time I wrote a letter to Maureen to give her a progress report on Piki. We had only gone as far as the second obedience session, and I was still unrealistically hopeful.

XIX.

A Thank You Letter

Northwest Academy of Canine Training
Seaview, Washington

Dear Maureen,

One day in April this year you generously gave to me, Jon Blumenthal, and a black dog named Pikachu from the WAIF shelter on Whidbey Island over an hour's worth of your time and expertise. I'm now giving you back an update, since you asked that I let you know how things worked out.

I officially took on foster care of Pikachu on Sunday evening, April 22. By Wednesday he voluntarily ran into his airline crate when I told him to "kennel up." As you might recall, this was for me the giant bugaboo about taking him on, since previous attempts to live-trap him in the wild had failed and he was terrified of coming close to any object of that boxy shape.

We have had our ups and downs since then—much too much to go into a lot of detail. Piki still has two different personalities: one on lead, one off. That includes being inside the house, as well as outside. When my husband looks in his direction, Piki still takes off for the far end of the house, although his acceptance of Curt is now sometimes better than others. He recently ran away, through my own inadvertent error.

We live across the street from a 300-foot-high cliff overlooking the Strait of Juan de Fuca, and I immediately determined that he had not gone over the cliff again (he is the only dog known in the neighborhood to have lived doing so and climbed back up by himself, without the aid of the volunteer fire department). By the next afternoon I found out that he had been seen in the dense woods behind a housing development about a mile from our home. I posted flyers with his photo and went door-to-door in the area handing them out. Was out one last time on Monday just before dark to blow my dog whistle (I had trained him to different signals on it) from the direction of our house when I found him about two blocks away, headed for home. Fortunately, I had my other resident dog along with me, and Piki was willing to come to Blue and eventually get into the car. He had gone wild again and wouldn't come directly to me. This happened just after I had enrolled him in an obedience class that was due to start ten days later. I did so because I didn't think his progress with my own obedience training was fast enough, and it lacked the necessary contact with other people and their dogs that he especially needs.

There have been many times in the last four months when I was ready to tear out my hair and turn Piki over to Jon Blumenthal to live forever with his pack of shelter rejects. I have often thought that paying you $1k would have been cheaper than replacing our carpet, but finally Piki is not spotting anymore unless he is surprised by a man coming into our house without any advance warning.

I know I am leaving many important aspects of his progress unsaid. Piki gets along well with our nine-year old Golden/Aussie mix, Blue, (whom we have only had for two years) and our three cats. He learns a lot from Blue and has, in turn, made a "real dog" of Blue, who had been trained to be a perfect little human boy in his previous life. Piki is very affectionate with me and occasionally so with Curt. I still feel there is great hope for him and so, at long last, I can tell you without reservation that he is doing well here.

We have a long way to go but it's thanks to you for your evaluation that we are very likely to make it as a family. We recently made our adoption of Pikachu official, so we are not likely to give up on him now.

Many heartfelt thanks, once again.

Best regards,
Barb Bland

XX.

Thanksgiving Runaway

November 22, 2001

On a gray and misty Thanksgiving morning, I took Piki and Blue for a long walk in the woods at Fort Ebey State Park. I wanted the dogs to be tired enough to sleep soundly while Curt and I, invited by friends for a holiday dinner, were out of the house later in the day.

I knew the risks of getting Piki back if I let him off lead, but I was so sure he was making progress that I took the chance anyhow.

Everything was going well. We had all walked briskly to the point where the Mainline trail branches off into the High Traverse and Alder Grove trails. Both dogs had run along just ahead of me, easily within catchable distance.

At the intersection of the trails, I turned back. Piki didn't.

At the last minute he had run on ahead and disappeared down one of the trails. Now any possible view of him was muffled by dripping gray-green shrubbery.

I blew our special *come* signal on my dog whistle until I was dizzy. Blue ran up as if to say, *Here I am, Mom,* but there was no Piki.

Furious at myself and at Piki, I turned my back on the trail intersection and started stomping my way back to the car. This was just too much. I had obligated myself to bring several dishes for a potluck Thanksgiving meal, and I simply didn't have more time to stay in the park. I *had* to go home to cook.

But by the time I reached the car and settled Blue into it, I was having fits of guilt. I cracked open the car windows and left Blue there so this older dog didn't have to do the same walk a second, tiring time. Then I ran the three-quarters of a mile all the way back to High Traverse, whistling and calling all the way.

No Piki.

When I turned back the second time, I was even more tired and angry, and even more short of time. He was still pulling these tricks after putting in several weeks in obedience school. *When* we were ever going to get on the same page?

Threatening aloud, I said through gritted teeth, "I'll come back for you at 3:00. If you don't come to me then, you live in the woods. If you come to your senses before 3:00, hang around."

On my way out of the park, I drove past the ranger's office and was surprised to see it was open. I told the ranger what had happened and that I would return at 3:00 p.m., an hour and a half before dark, to try again to find Piki.

I returned home a little after 11:30 and started cooking immediately, all the while thinking only of Pikachu. How could I get enough accomplished to go back to the park at 3:00? I worked like a madwoman. I would only have from 3:00 until 4:30 to find him. At this time of year it would be black-dark before 5:00, and, besides, that was the time we were supposed to leave home for our friends' house.

A little before 3:00, I told Curt how to manage the dishes in the oven, threw off my apron, and slipped into my hiking boots, jacket, hat, and gloves. Blue stayed home. His old hips had been exercised enough for one day.

I parked the car at the end of the Mainline trail, in the same spot as the morning, and set off running east on Mainline, intent upon returning to the intersection of trails where we separated as a starting place.

I felt very lonely as I stood there to catch my breath, puffing clouds of steam in the low overcast. I whistled and shouted for Piki, but I knew there would be no response. It felt empty. Only the trees and shrubs heard me.

What now?

Piki had been gone almost four hours on his own. He had probably gone back to the car to look for us. After that he might have gone south over to the Kettles trail, roughly parallel to Mainline, but a generous half-mile south of it. It was a better-known trail and there were bound to be more people walking there, to work up an appetite or to work off a heavy meal. Not that he would need to be with people he didn't know, but it was worth a try. He might be looking for me there.

The nearby Boundary trail ran north and south between Mainline and Kettles. It was the quickest way for me to get over to Kettles and, it crossed the trail area of the park like the line of a diameter through a circle. If I kept on using the dog whistle *come* signal on Boundary, the loud, shrill sound might carry to the other, closer trails on the perimeter.

I ran south on Boundary, stopping frequently to whistle and to listen for any response. Arriving at Kettles, I did the same as I walked eastward, finally turning north on the Alder Grove trail to circle back to the same intersection where we had parted in the morning. I covered those three trails and the result was the same: nothing, nothing, and nothing.

By this time, I was definitely walking, no longer running. I went west again to Boundary and this time, I turned north. I climbed the hills to the northern limit of Boundary and turned east, circling back to High Traverse and Mainline. By now, I must have covered at least four miles since I'd left the car. Darkness was falling like heavy eyelids. I didn't have much time left.

I took one more sweep south on Boundary, frantically blowing my whistle as loudly as I could. I planned to go only halfway to Kettles before I turned back because if I went all the way, it would be completely dark by the time I returned to the car.

Mostly out of breath and nearly out of hope, I whistled only occasionally as I walked through the tunnel of trees on my final return to Mainline.

Suddenly, I froze, hearing something rustling in the underbrush about a hundred feet ahead of me on the trail. It was almost too dark to distinguish what the something black hurtling toward me was. Then I saw its white toes and white chest.

"Piki!" I shrieked. I knelt and held out my arms.

I've been looking everywhere for you, he seemed to say, as he wagged his tail, and bumped into me, nearly knocking me over.

I hugged and petted him. He licked my face, genuinely happy to find me, acting as if I had been lost and he had done every possible thing to find me.

Together we hurried home.

I'm sure Piki slept soundly while Curt and I were at our party.

Actually, I slept pretty soundly while Curt and I were at our party.

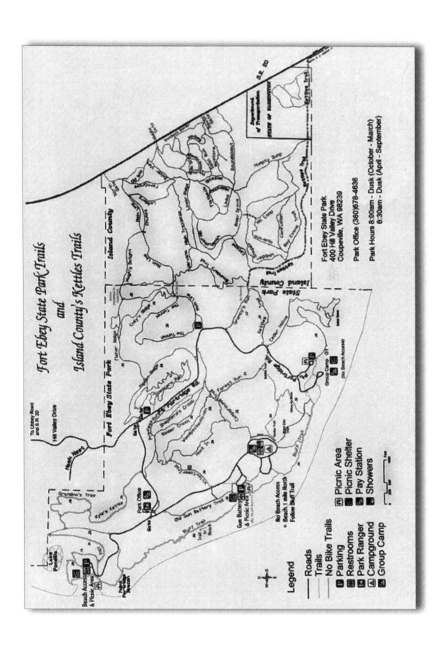

Part Four

Trial and Error

XXI.

Pre-Agility School

November 2001 – January 2002

In Piki's first experience with obedience school, I didn't get much helpful instruction about how to correct his unruly inattentiveness or lack of appreciation for food rewards.

Nobody had seemed to know what to do with him. Saying the word *no* was highly discouraged. Piki was the class clown and a disruptive influence, but the teacher tried to ignore it. This class for dog owners was based on the same theory of permissiveness that had invaded and conquered the public school systems about the time Curt and I retired from teaching. The only strategy presented was rewards. Punishment was forbidden, and correction equaled punishment.

Although Piki knew exactly how to behave with other dogs, he did not know how to behave with humans or how to meet their expectations. He needed more structure and less go-with-the-flow.

Needless to say, Piki never made much progress in this class, though we had toughed it out to the end.

Imagine our classmates' dismay, then, when we enrolled in the next course offered to the same group, a pre-agility class. I thought that maybe Piki would do better in this endeavor because of his working-dog genes. Accomplishing these tasks was based on the same motivation-reward pattern as obedience commands, but it involved different activities. Piki was smart and athletic, and Border Collies, bonded with their masters, often excel at meeting the challenge of agility courses. The key phrase here is *bonded with their masters*. Piki and I were not bonded. Not yet.

Just as I expected, Piki was quite capable of accomplishing the tasks put forward: walking on narrow boards raised off the floor, jumping fences, climbing to the top of stairs and down the other side, balancing on a teeter-board. And he was not, thank God, the only dog in class to enter a tunnel and then hide inside it, refusing to exit at either end. We were never allowed to attempt the weave-poles because this required Piki to be off-lead for a sustained length of time. Still, we learned a great deal.

What Piki could not tolerate about pre-agility class was the use of clickers as a reward.

The winner of an agility competition perfectly performs on a sequence of required apparatuses in the fastest possible time. No time now for hugs or verbal praise or even food treats as rewards. These may take only seconds, but that's too long, as the dog is required to move on to the next piece of equipment immediately. We had graduated to teaching the dogs that their desired goal was hearing an instant click sound made with a small handheld metal device.

We started to teach this transition by putting a single small treat inside a clean dog food can and placing this at the finishing end of an apparatus. The seconds it takes for the dog to stop and eat the treat create a pause—just an instant—when the dog looks to his handler for direction to the next challenge. This pause is required in a judged competition. In training, the handler gives a click at the same time the dog eats the treat. Over time, the dog comes to identify the click as the reward, and the edible treat is removed.

For Piki, however, this system was not ideal. He had long been terrified by unexpected noises. This was a lifelong holdover of the self-defense mechanisms that had allowed him to survive on his own as a pup in the wild. Whether these unexpected sounds were subtle or loud, soft or sharp, he shied away from them. In the same way as a gun-shy dog will do, Piki heard the clicks and refused to work. He wanted only to get away from the sound.

An assistant-teacher suggested that I ditch the dreaded clicker, and in its place, enthusiastically hiss a single word *yessss!* when Piki accomplished his task. Surprisingly, this worked well, and Piki liked it.

When we did our daily walks on the beach, I had Piki prance along the tops of driftwood logs, pausing at the end of one before jumping to the next one. *Yessss.* In our yard at home I put together our old Golden Retriever's graduated jumps and we practiced with them. *Yessss.* My husband removed a bi-fold closet door, covered one side of it with outdoor carpet to provide traction, and balanced it on a fulcrum so Piki could practice the teeter-board. *Yessss.* I begged a discarded refrigerator shipping box from the local appliance store to use as a shorter tunnel-trainer. *Yessss. Yessss. Yessss.* Piki was having fun and so was I. Even Blue participated in the easier challenges.

With the rest of the class, we advanced to working on cold January nights in a huge horse barn. At first, the strange, strong horsey smells and dim lighting of this new location spooked Piki. He still had trouble trusting that I wouldn't lead him into danger. And I had trouble trusting that he wouldn't run away, as the training required much more time off lead. Eventually, what made him run for the exits were the clicks intended for other dogs in the cavernous arena.

It seemed that performing all the required tasks in familiar, safe surroundings was fine fun, but adapting his skills to new circumstances was more than Piki could handle.

So, he had learned a lot, but Pre-Agility School was not for us, either.

XXII.

Night Runaway

January 2002

One dark January morning around five o'clock, I let Blue out in the backyard to do his business. I slid open the deck door, flipped on the outside light, and stood inside the house to watch him. He made quick work of it and dashed back to the deck to re-enter the house and go back to bed. I dashed right back to bed after him.

But then I realized that Piki had to go out, too. Not daring to let him outside alone, I went to the front entryway closet to find my parka, boots, and a flashlight. In a sleepy fog, I fumbled with attaching to Piki's collar a twenty-foot retractable leash, the only leash that was at hand. Usually he used a long woven-cloth leash. He was jumping up and down by now, eager to get outside, and I was clumsy, juggling a coat, a flashlight, and a leash while opening the storm door, all the while trying to be quiet enough not to wake Curt.

Retractable leashes are spring-loaded wire cables attached to a large, plastic-covered spool within a handle. The handle is designed with an opening large enough to accommodate a fist clutching the grip. It has a trigger device to release or lock the cable in place so that it can be extended to any length, then locked in place, or retracted and locked.

Piki burst out the door ahead of me, dragging the cable to its twenty-foot limit and jerking the leash right out of my hand. He seemed as surprised as I was when the plastic handle clanked to the sidewalk.

I doubt that he really intended to run away but, frightened by the unexpected noise, that is exactly what he did. Piki galloped away to the north, a black streak in a black night, dragging the frantically clattering leash behind him.

I was sure the dog was headed toward the big field where he had emerged from the woods after his extended August weekend escape. It was a convenient place to walk, and we sometimes would go there after breakfast or before bedtime.

As the dog streaked out of sight, I knew I should go after him right away. What if he actually went into the woods again and got the leash cable caught on the trees or the ground cover!

I ran to the corner. It was hard for me to distinguish anything in the deep darkness. I couldn't see or hear Piki anywhere. When the occasional early morning car went by, I ducked down out of the range of the headlights so that the glaring white edges of my bathrobe didn't attract the driver's attention.

Standing out there wondering what to do next was pointless. After a few minutes, I reluctantly went home, dressed in street clothes, and lay down once again on the living room couch. I set an alarm clock for first daylight. The alarm blasted me into consciousness just before seven o'clock. Curt wasn't up yet. I wrote him a note, took my morning pills, and gobbled some toast and cheese, not knowing how long I'd be out. In my parka and boots, I set out for the field, all the while saying my prayers for heavenly help.

As I neared the meadow, I stopped and surveyed it from the distance. Black trees bordered it on the east and north. The broad, open expanse of grassy stubble reflected the cloudy dawn's pearly light.

But, wait a minute. As I got closer, something was different about the meadow this time. Near the far north end, almost a quarter mile away, there was something new, something I had never noticed before. It was low to the ground, black, unmoving. I really couldn't make out from this distance what it was, but it seemed a good starting place for my search.

I shouted and whistled, "Piki" as I ran toward it.

It didn't move.

I rushed forward, straining to identify what this was, finding it curious that if it was my dog and he was unmoving, possibly injured, or worse, he was curled up in a ball, in a normal sleeping position, not sprawled out on his side with his head and limbs spread away from his torso.

As I got closer, I was relieved to see a head rise up from this black body-bundle. The eyes looked woefully toward me. Thank God, as the head rose up from its body, I could see the white tuxedo shirt on its black chest. His tail thumped slowly.

"Piki! What happened to you? Are you all right?" I gasped, as I reached him and knelt beside him.

His tail wagged a little faster and he slowly stood up, his head still low.

I hugged him and touched him all over, probing to see if he was hurt. He seemed to be badly demoralized, but not physically injured. I followed his eyes in the dim light as he turned his head to glance at the dreaded, still-attached retractable leash, dangling next to him on the ground.

Picking up the handle, I released the tension, and stood up, reassuring Piki that the terrifying object sticking to him like a shadow would no longer clatter along, following his every move.

As we walked back home, I marveled that I had found him so easily and quickly. But, as I continued to think about it, I realized that he had intended to make that possible.

Emotionally exhausted from the terror of the hated leash that had clung to him like a curse, Piki must have noticed that when he stopped moving, it also stopped. So, if he lay down and tried to sleep, he could wait for me to come for him.

Clearly, he chose an open place where I *could* find him. It was as if he were certain that I would come looking for him, counted on me to rescue him. After all, it had always happened before—the August weekend he ran away from home, Thanksgiving Day in the cold, rainy woods, initially finding him at Teronda West and bringing him back to the shelter.

As we walked home in the growing daylight, I assured him that I would never again use the retractable leash.

And I felt a deepening sense of warmth in the realization that he needed me, trusted me, *wanted* to be with me.

XXIII.

Invisible Fence

January – February 2002

A few mornings after Piki's latest runaway, while I was reading the newspaper at breakfast, my eyes came to rest on an advertisement for the Invisible Fence. I'm sure I'd glanced over this same ad dozens of other mornings, but at this magic moment I *saw* it.

This would be the answer to letting Pikachu outside in the yard with Blue. With crystal clarity I saw that I didn't want to continue our middle-of-the-night rambles forever.

I knew only vaguely how a barrier like this works. A live electrical wire is buried a few inches underground around the outer limits of the area to be enclosed. The dog wears a collar tuned to receive transmitted signals from the wire at any time when the dog ventures too close to it or crosses over it.

I remembered uncomfortably the rainy, dark winter evening when I had seen a dog running down the road in my neighborhood, his frightened eyes reflecting the headlights and the bulge of an electrical receiver mechanism in his collar. I now realized that this dog had crossed the line, receiving a shock but escaping from his invisibly fenced area. If he then tried to return to his yard, he would receive yet another shock. And if the owners had relied solely on confining the dog to his yard and didn't educate him about how to handle the outside world, he would be helpless, overwhelmed, and terrified. That would be a major problem!

I told myself to settle down, not to get carried away by my negative speculation on the subject. There had to be knowledgeable people around who could advise me about pros and cons of the invisible fence.

Later that morning, I called a local veterinarian to get his opinion: "I'm considering getting an invisible fence for my dogs. I hear horror stories about it. Can you tell me if it's safe?"

"It is," he said, "if you buy it directly from the Invisible Fence Company, which trains you to use it." He added that the patent had expired a few years earlier and the idea had been widely copied. "Now people buy it in hardware stores, and they never learn how to properly use it. They hurt their dogs with the shock and blame the product."

That was enough information for me. I phoned the number in the Invisible Fence advertisement and introduced myself to the installers: Ned and his wife, Betty. A few days later Ned and Betty came to our house for a screening appointment. Before they would commit to installing the fence, they insisted on meeting Curt and me and seeing our yard and animals to evaluate whether or not we were proper candidates for this technology.

We began with a tour of the front and back yards, and then I took the couple inside to meet my husband, Blue, Piki, and the cats: Tessa, Puck, and Halo. I had explained that Piki was the issue and the reason we were asking for their services, so their questions focused on him.

Betty asked, "How long have you had Piki?"

"I brought him home from the shelter last April, but because I was a volunteer there, I've known him since he was a pup." I hit the highlights of Piki's background at the shelter and his various escapes.

"And he's how old?" Ned questioned.

"Two."

"He seems to get along well with the cats and the other dog."

"He adores Blue. He's afraid of Tessa, so he doesn't chase the cats. Puck and Halo couldn't care less about him. Do you have dogs and cats?"

Ned and Betty had just gotten a third dog—a stray that had crawled, hurt and malnourished, into their yard. "He knew he needed help," Ned said, "but he was afraid to get it."

I told them that Piki had been on his own in Central Whidbey from between the ages of eight months and thirteen months. "That's when I caught him," I said. "I took him back to the shelter. But I wound up with him, after all."

"It takes a lot of time and patience to get them to trust you."

"But it's so much more rewarding than the easy ones."

We all laughed. We obviously had a lot in common. We traded animal stories for another half-hour by which time it was apparent that Ned and Betty had come to a silent agreement: we'd be suitable for the installation as long as we promised to follow the prescribed training routine.

I told Ned exactly where I wanted the wire in the yards, front and back. He dug narrow, shallow trenches and buried the wire around the perimeter of the yards. Once he'd finished, he stuck wires with small white flags into the ground about four feet inside the wire's perimeter and ten feet apart. The fluttering white flag clearly marked how close a dog could come to the wire before its collar would set off a beeping sound as a warning. If the dog lingered near the wire or actually crossed it, the dog would get it in the neck. Literally.

One thing I had learned while volunteering at the shelter was to try every new piece of equipment on myself before I put it on a dog. I wanted to know, firsthand, what the dog was experiencing. Now, I walked around the edges of the yard with the collar in my hand, bent over so that I was roughly Piki's height and could be sure to hear its *beep beep beep*.

Then I pressed the signal-receiving prongs of the collar tightly against my thigh and moved closer to the fence. *Zap!*

Ouch!

Not a knockout shock. In fact, not even enough to cause real pain. But impressive, nonetheless. It was enough of a jolt to get my attention.

With Ned and Betty watching, I snapped the invisible fence collar around Piki's neck and began to walk him around the yard on a long lead, repeatedly letting him wander close enough to the flags to hear the *beep* and then rushing him back to safety toward the center of the yard or toward the house.

The big question for me was what to do if he got out anyhow? What if Piki crossed the line and got the shock—how would he get back into the yard without getting shocked again?

There were only two answers: remove the collar and return across the line, or disconnect the electricity until he's safely back in the yard.

We all expected this training to take some time for Piki, Curt, and me to get used to it. Ned and Betty left us with an illustrated training manual, a video training tape, and the phone number of an on-call assistant who lived closer to us than they did. They said the assistant would drop in periodically over the next few weeks to see how we were doing and answer questions. They also said that after we—humans and animals—became familiar with the location of the flags, we could remove them. Then the wire would truly be invisible.

We practiced several times each day when Piki left the house for potty outings. I let him roam on his twenty-foot lead until he'd gotten close enough to the white flags to hear the beep. Then, I said, "Come" firmly and began to pull him toward me as I ran backward in the direction of the house— to safety.

This training carried a huge bonus. Piki learning to stay within the limits of the yard, at the same time he was also progressing on learning to *come*—something he had failed miserably in his obedience class.

This was working so well that, simultaneously, we added practicing *come* on the long lead inside the house.

And he GOT it! *Yesssss!* He realized that *come* on the long-lead actually meant *come directly to me, right now. Come toward the house. Come into the house.* Just plain *come* — the hardest command to teach a dog.

After just a few days, I could stand on the deck watching, leash in hand, while Piki and Blue romped in the yard together, unfettered by leashes. Then came the day when the warning flags were removed. My heart in my throat, I continued to watch from the yard or the deck door because there were always temptations to bolt: people walking and jogging on the road, especially other dogs and their masters. He might be wary of new people, but Piki was always interested in other dogs.

He did cross the wire. Twice. But because I was watching, I was able to pull the plug on the electricity and go right out after him. He didn't get far.

I had been a slow-learner about so many things in dealing with Piki. In the process, my brain had been seared by certain truths: all dogs are not the same—different approaches work for different dogs. You have to have the right equipment. But you have to know how to use it properly because the equipment doesn't magically work by itself. Dogs can jump fences; they can dig out under them. Dogs can learn to open gates and doors. Collars and leashes are not foolproof. All of these aids must be used correctly. There is no substitute for direct supervision.

And sometimes even that doesn't work.

XXIV.

Anniversary Syndrome

August 3-5, 2002

Curt walked the dogs on the first Saturday morning in August 2002 because I was busy doing housework. As I washed windows, I had a nagging feeling that they were gone longer than usual. When he and Blue finally burst in through the door from the garage into the dining room, Curt's face looked pale and he was agitated.

"I lost him!" he exclaimed. "Piki got away from me."

"Where?"

"Near the back entrance to Fort Ebey."

"What happened?" If there's one thing I can't tolerate, it's standing by idly when action can and should be taken: I was already reaching for my sneakers to get ready to go after Piki.

"I parked the car at the back gate. We walked and then, when I opened the door for the dogs to get back in to come home, I took the leash off Piki's collar and he just stood there. He wouldn't get in the car."

Curt sank into a chair. "I shouldn't have taken off his leash until after he was in the car, I know," he looked at me, expecting me to tell him exactly that, beating me to the punch.

Having been through all that myself when Piki went over the cliff, what could I say?

"So, he went back into the woods?"

"He didn't go anywhere. He just stood nearby, out of reach. I didn't know what to do, so I drove away, slowly. Piki followed the car, but when I stopped to open the door for him, he shied away."

"And then?"

"I drove from the park up to where the road joins West Beach Road. Piki followed all the way, but when we got close to the road and he saw other cars, they scared him. I tried again, but he wouldn't get into the car. Then, something else frightened him and he ran into a wheat field on the west side of the road. I came straight home to tell you."

Curt and I drove directly back to where Piki had disappeared. We parked the car on the side road and walked around the area, whistling and calling for the dog. A man came out of his house and asked whom we were calling for. When we told him "a medium-sized black dog," the man shouted, "I saw him about thirty minutes ago. He ran toward the park," he said, pointing in a southwesterly direction. He added that there were two big, menacing dogs that live near the wheat field that no doubt urged Piki to move on.

We drove the streets of the Sierra subdivision, through which Piki would have had to pass to return to the tall trees at the back entrance of the park. Curt drove slowly, peering out the left side of the car. I searched for Piki on the right side, whistling and calling for him through the open car window.

Nothing.

We were running out of gas, so Curt left to refill the tank while I continued to walk around Sierra.

No response.

Soon, Curt returned for me and we went home. I needed to get to work on reporting Piki lost. There was last year's flyer to update . . .

Last year!

Suddenly, the day's date dawned on me: Saturday, August 3.

As if the planets' annual alignment had triggered some tiny memory cell in Piki's brain, he was gone again. Just as he had been on August 5, when he escaped from his original owner during the first year of his life, and again squeezed through our deck door and escaped into the woods on August 4 during his second year.

During the previous week I had caught myself wondering if a third annual escape would happen again this year. Well, it did.

These strange annual vibrations were as dramatic and noticeable as the ones in play in January 2001 when, after months of impasse, Jigglypuff and Starmie were adopted and Pikachu captured. All within ten days.

I phoned WAIF to report that Piki was lost. Then I rushed into town to get to the local newspaper office while it was still open to submit a lost ad for Piki. The women in the ad department knew me well from having handled the WAIF advertisements in recent years and they were helpful. They suggested that I pay extra to show a photograph of Piki and to have the ad printed in all the area-wide small town newspapers operated by Sound Publications. They argued successfully that every summer the state parks on Whidbey Island are very busy and popular with area-wide tourists, as well as those from around the world.

Of course, the problem with Piki would continue to be that even when found, he would most likely come only to me.

I hurried back home, updated last year's flyers, sealed them in ziplock plastic bags, and returned to the park to post them. I was careful to post a flyer near the unofficial back entrance to the park, used most often only by local residents.

And then I waited. And waited. And spent another fitful Saturday night.

I got up at 5:30 Sunday morning, fed Blue, had a bite to eat, and put Blue in the car and set off for a new area to search.

What if Piki had not gone to the park after all, or had not stayed there, as we believed from the man who pointed out the southwesterly direction that Piki had originally taken? There was another largely wooded area on the east side of West Beach Road, not too far from the park: Roberts Pond.

We drove as far as we could on the road that had been recently cut in for the area's housing development before we started walking. I called and whistled for Piki. The early morning swallows, darting through the sky above us, answered. Blue walked beside me through the tall and dewy grass. But there was no Piki.

Later in the day I returned to the park to try to find him. The dilemma was that he was torn between wanting to be with people, yet fearing those with whom he was not familiar. So should I look for him close to the campgrounds or in the more remote places?—which were everywhere else.

I carried a flyer with me and showed it to a few campers.

"Any chance you've seen this dog hanging around?"

"No. Sorry," was the uniform answer.

I was tired and defeated. I felt very sorry for my poor dog, who had now not eaten for two days and nights. I felt very sorry for myself. And I was angry that Piki had brought this misery on himself and me—yet again.

I went home and slept.

I did not get an early start on Monday.

Blue and I took our morning walk in the park, half-heartedly looking once again for Piki or anyone who might have seen him.

Many of the weekend campers had packed up and left. There were not nearly as many people to ask. And we knew what the answer would be. I was giving up hope.

Early in the afternoon Curt hit upon an idea.

"Did you post the flyers in the park bathrooms?" he asked.

"Never even thought of it," I brightened. "I'll phone the ranger right away to try to get his permission."

The long-suffering park ranger, who knew me and my work with WAIF because we had worked together a couple times to help pets that were lost or abandoned in the park, answered the phone himself.

"This time it's my own dog," I pleaded. "He's been gone since Saturday morning and we think he's hiding out in the park."

"I've seen your flyers," the ranger replied, sympathetically.

"My husband just thought of posting them in the bathrooms. Would you let me do that? I'll take them down as soon as we get him."

"Yeah, I guess so. We don't usually let people do it, but I know it's probably your best chance."

I printed more flyers, and Curt and I drove to the park. Curt posted them in the men's rooms, I in the ladies' rooms. We each taped them to the bathroom mirrors and hurried back home to sit by the telephone.

Within a half-hour our phone jangled. The man on the other end spoke with a heavy German accent.

My hope soared. Having been raised in a community with a strong German influence, I knew how much the Germans adore dogs.

"Ja. I zaw your dok. He's been hanging arount our campsite all veekend, but ve didn't know he vas lost."

"Where is your campsite in the park?"

He gave me the number and location.

"Thanks so much. I'll be right there."

Piki was nowhere to be found when we got to the campsite, but hope of finding him was strong again: we knew with certainty that he was in the park and trying to make contact with people.

Blue and I took our late afternoon walk on the trails near the campground, me yelling "Pikachu" and blowing the familiar *come* call on my dog whistle. The first trail we took was the Pacific Northwest Trail around Lake Pondilla. No response. We retraced our steps to the road leading from the back park entrance and began again.

This time, instead of turning right to descend to the lake on the PNT, we went straight, soon passing the intersection of the Kyle's Kettle trail where we often walked.

Blue stopped and stood still, turning his head to the left, toward the trail.

A black nose appeared around the edge of a curve in the trail. Then, cautiously, an eye. Half a head.

With a rush that tumbled stones down the trail, Piki scrambled down to us, jumping, whining, wagging, barking: *I'm here, I'm here.*

"Piki!" I shouted.

Blue wagged his whole body.

In an extravagant greeting ceremony, the three of us hugged and kissed each other. I knelt and stroked both dogs, holding them tight. Piki snuggled against my legs and licked Blue's face, then mine. He eagerly sat, wanting to be put on his leash.

After three long days of constant searching, Piki had once again finally succeeded in finding us.

XXV.

Vacation Plans

September 6-7, 2002

For several years in the 1990s, Curt and I had enjoyed playing in an annual golf tournament on the Oregon Coast during the week after Labor Day. After the tournament folded, we continued to vacation in different places on the coast at that time of the year. I knew that my sister would enjoy it, too, and she had never visited Oregon so we invited her to join us there for a week in 2002. We all planned to meet at the same hotel in Portland on Monday, September 9, to spend a few days seeing the city and then drive to a time-share in Depoe Bay that Curt and I had arranged for the rest of the week.

Martha had made her airline reservations. I had booked a boarding facility for Piki and Blue for the week, planning to deliver them on Sunday evening so that we could leave early Monday to drive to Portland. These long-standing plans being made, I walked the dogs at Rocky Point, a beach on the nearby Navy base, on the Friday evening preceding our trip.

When it came time for Piki and Blue to get into the car to return home after our walk late on Friday afternoon, I made the same mistake Curt had made almost exactly a month earlier at Fort Ebey Park. I opened the car door and Blue jumped in. I unhooked Piki's leash and expected him to jump in, as well.

Instead, he backed away, just out of reach, tilting his head and looking at me with mischief in his eyes.

Come back for me Tuesday, he seemed to be saying.

"Like hell! You come with me right now. Get in the car."

He danced away.

We had walked a little later than usual that evening, and the autumn sun was setting earlier and earlier. Piki's black coat barely contrasted with the dusk.

"You miserable devil dog. Get your buns back into that car right now."

Piki spied a rabbit near the wild rose bushes and charged after it.

"That's it, buster."

This was getting so old! I couldn't believe that I had blown it again. Or that he was still pulling this stunt. Furious, I slammed shut the open door, climbed into the driver's seat, started the car and stepped on the gas. Blue and I peeled away in a screeching shower of gravel and dust.

But by the time I got to the firing range, then the golf course, I could only think of the resident coyotes and a dumped dog in that area I had once tried to catch after I saw it abandoned by its owner. It wouldn't come near me that night, but when I went to get it at first light the next morning, it was only too happy to run to me after its sleepless night of terror.

I was too proud and too angry to admit defeat by driving back the route I had taken to leave. I circled around to make Piki think it was a different car arriving in the parking lot. I could see him standing, alert, in the distance. Naturally, he recognized the sound of the car. Then he casually dropped his head, sniffing the ground with total indifference to me. It made me furious all over again and I drove away, this time without returning.

I spent the night brooding: what would I do if I didn't catch Piki by Sunday? Send Curt to meet Martha in Oregon without me? Somehow catch up with them later in the week after I caught Piki? Or have both of us stay home until we caught Piki, then figure out what to do about Martha and the rest of our trip?

I knew there was no possible way I could leave home and enjoy a vacation without first getting Piki back.

Early the next morning I revised the lost-dog flyers for the umpteenth time and set out to post them around Rocky Point. I put them at Joseph Whidbey Park, too. We always drove to either location and walked only there, so Piki wouldn't have reason to know they were connected, but I thought he might wander down that way.

I wore Blue out walking around Rocky Point in the morning, then left him at home and went back alone in the afternoon. This time I parked the car at Joseph Whidbey Park, the site of Starmie's escape, and worked my way north along the path between the ocean and the marsh, toward Rocky Point. Piki, Blue, and I walked here at least four afternoons a week, so Piki would certainly feel at home here if he came down this way.

I got close to the boundary between the two recreation areas, calling and whistling, as always, when there was a noisy splash in the marsh and Piki burst out of it, onto the trail. He looked startled to see that I was so close by. With no intention to come to me, he started to sprint past. I stuck out my arm into his path and he ran right into it. I didn't care if I ripped the fur off his back! I had him. And I wasn't letting go.

Chagrinned, he wagged weakly and lowered his head for me to attach a leash. I felt very pleased that this torment had ended in a timely manner and I didn't have to worry about our trip anymore.

Strolling toward the car, we saw a fellow dog walker who was new to me. He looked at us keenly from the distance, marched up to us and said, "This is the dog on the poster at the trailhead."

"Indeed it is," I said.

"I'm Terry," he said, "and this is Frasier." He pointed at his Jack Russell terrier. "We were just coming to look for him."

"I'm Barb, and this is Pikachu, the escape artist, the runner, the dog who professes not to know right from wrong or good from bad."

"He looks nice enough to me."

Piki and Frasier were noses-to-noses and getting acquainted.

"Can I say hello to him?"

"He's very shy with new people, especially guys. Let me kneel behind him so he can't squirm away from you. Most people think he should come up to them, but he will never do that; you have to come to him and I have to keep him from worming his way out of it. He's got to know that not everyone is going to hurt him."

"I hate to force my attention on anyone who doesn't want it."

"But that's exactly what you have to do. And you're actually doing him a favor. He'll be a better person for it."

Terry squatted with Piki between us and gently stroked him.

Piki must have known that he was in good hands because he hardly resisted.

This was the first of many happy meetings with Terry and Frasier. Terry was the first man that Piki ever sought out from a distance and ran to greet.

XXVI.

Wag 'n' Walk

September 25, 2002

Not long after our return from Oregon, a growing rumble of publicity began for the third annual Wag 'n' Walk WAIF fundraiser. It was to be held at the end of September at an off-leash dog park on Central Whidbey. Wag 'n' Walk was an afternoon celebration of animal shelter alumni and their adopters, presenting a wonderful opportunity to see and be-seen and to enjoy the happily-ever-after stories of the dogs.

It was hard to even recognize some dogs with their Forever Owners, they were so different from their shelter-selves: happy, relaxed, confident, they actually looked different.

Vendors set up booths to offer pet-related products. Public address system static crackled as dogs and their owners participated in contests. Color and noise, waves of laughter, *ooohs* and *aaahs* spread among the crowds. Camera shutters clicked. Dogs were on their best behavior, knowing they were the featured performers: the spotlight was on them.

The highlight of the festival was the crowning of two former shelter dogs chosen as King and Queen for the day. These dogs were selected by judging 500-word essays written by their owners about how their WAIF companion had added to their lives. Substantial prizes made it worth the effort to compete.

Our WAIF dog, Blue, had a dramatic story of his own, but added to Piki's, I felt that it was interesting enough to submit for the contest:

> Blue was the happy resident dog of an adult family nursing home when he fell upon hard times. He watched at his beloved owner's bedside as she died slowly of cancer. Instead of going to the new home his owner had designated, an unauthorized employee insisted upon keeping him. She neglected the patients and destroyed the business, but continued to live in the house. Several months went by. Water and electricity were shut off. When the bank foreclosed, the assistant Animal Control Officer and the bankers slipped their feet and legs into heavy-duty trash bags to enter the house. They found Blue confined inside, matted with feces. Although he had been fed, he had not been outside in the length of time it took for his claws to grow long and curl under.

> The people specified to take Blue after his owner's death now declined because they feared that he couldn't possibly be housebroken any longer. So Blue made a trip to the groomer and then to the shelter. The night of his arrival at our house, I paraded Blue outside every few hours. He was obviously relieved not to have to do his business inside the house.

> Over the next few days we were amazed to see his impeccable manners. He never begged for food, got along perfectly with the cats, never even stuck his nose inside

a bathroom. On our walks, he paced behind me like Prince Phillip to the Queen: the "perfect little boy"—most un-doglike.

After happily settling into his new life, Blue got an awful jolt when, in 2001, we brought home Pikachu, a semi-feral dog, from the shelter to foster. Blue was no longer the centerpiece and only dog. Moreover, Piki was everything Blue was not: a teenage delinquent with a sweet disposition, but otherwise unsocialized, unruly, unfriendly, and unhousebroken. Afraid of everyone and everything. And unwilling to learn to try to please.

That's where Blue proved invaluable. When we wanted Piki to learn a new behavior, Blue willingly modeled it for him. Piki observed and decided that if Blue enthusiastically did what we asked, it was OK for him to do it, too. After more than a year, we've had our ups and downs with Piki, but we couldn't possibly have made the progress with him that we did if it hadn't been for Blue.

Thanks to Blue, we've been able to give two shelter dogs a chance for a good life in a happy family pack. They have added so much to our lives. We have enjoyed them and learned from them, as they have from one another. We now understand that dogs have more influence over each other than people have influence over them. Piki has learned trust and confidence and some manners from Blue: Blue has learned to forge ahead in walks, to enjoy splashing in puddles and get dirty, to chase and wrestle with Piki, and to be a doggy-dog—as well as the best-behaved, friendly, loving pet that anyone could ask for.

Shortly after noon on the last Sunday in September, I got ready to leave for the dog park south of Coupeville. Piki and Blue were resting from their morning walk and I wondered how I could get Blue to come to the door without Piki tagging along. After his recent series of escapes, I was sure that I must have been fooling myself to think he had made any progress at all. If Piki came along with us to Wag 'n' Walk, I expected him to be uncontrollably freaky among all the people and commotion at the dog park and I didn't think I could manage both dogs alone.

It was the first time I asked something of one of them without including the other. Piki was understandably confused when I put a leash on Blue and tried to slip out the dining room door to the garage with only him. From inside, Piki could hear Blue get into the car, the overhead door open and me slipping into the driver's seat. Before I could start the engine, I heard him jumping up and down inside the dining room, his paws clawing at the door. He was whining pitifully, begging to go along. He had no idea what he'd be getting into. He was better off staying home.

The pleading to go with us grew stronger.

OK, he could come. But he just might find himself spending the afternoon in the car.

I never dreamed that Piki would wind up having the best time of any of us.

We rolled up to the park and I braced myself to turn a deaf ear to Piki, telling him simply that he had to wait in the car while Blue and I got out.

Blue's eyes widened as we approached several acres of dogs and their people. We checked in at the registration table and walked toward the WAIF booth, greeting old friends and volunteers.

"Hey, Blue, you handsome boy. How're ya doin'?"

"He doesn't even look like the same person!"

"Gosh, he looks good. Where's Pikachu?"

"He's in the car. I didn't know how he would react to all these people. He's still pretty spooky around people he doesn't know, especially guys."

"Here, I'll hold Blue for you. Bring Piki out. We've got to see him."

Blue gazed after me as I handed his leash to a friend and headed for the car.

Piki could see me coming and, behind me, the booths and milling crowd. When I snapped on his leash and he jumped out of the car, Piki was clearly stunned at the level of noise and activity that the car had muffled, but he bravely walked beside me toward the commotion without trying to shy away.

It took me a minute to figure out why. Then I got it: Piki didn't see any people at all; he focused only on their dogs. This was too good to be true... all these interesting dogs, in one place.

Tail high, legs stiff, he stalked up to the nearest dog to sniff hello.

"Look at him. He's beautiful."

"He's all filled out. Not that raw-boned teeny-bopper anymore."

"Look at the muscles. Wow."

Just then, a woman's voice rang out on a microphone, "Time to announce the winners of the contest for King and Queen. Will all the contestants line up over here for the grand march, please?"

"I've got to get Blue," I said. "I've entered him in the contest for King."

"Here, let us take Piki. We'll take care of him while you and Blue do your thing."

Hesitating a little, I turned Piki's leash over to two volunteers that Piki had never met before. As Blue and I walked away, I looked back to see, thankfully, that they had Piki interacting with three other dogs. He didn't even notice that they were petting him at the same time because he was so pleasantly distracted.

When I saw the capes and crowns that the King and Queen had to wear, I was relieved that we didn't win! Blue took second place and pranced beside me in the grand march, unencumbered. His prize was to have his picture taken by a professional photographer who was present at the event.

Once the grand march was over, I retrieved Piki and linked the two dogs together on one leash with a small leather tandem clasp that hooked into both their collars. I met the photographer in a quiet, wooded area off to the side of the activities. Piki was leery of her, but he couldn't get away without dragging Blue along. The best he could do was to lie at Blue's feet and pretend someone wasn't pointing a camera at him. The photo of the two dogs turned out beautifully and I treasure it. The photographer also took a lovely picture of Blue alone.

Our duties accomplished, the dogs got a big drink of water. We sat down in the grass near friends, talked and relaxed. Excitement and stress had tired the dogs out. They were happy to have a break and some quiet time.

A man I had never met and his dog came over to talk with someone in our group. The dog bent over Piki and nuzzled him. The man squatted down and gently stroked Piki's flank as he chatted. Piki was unruffled, acting like it was an everyday occurrence to be petted by a stranger. A man, at that.

To me, it was a revelation: I realized that Piki didn't have to be totally dependent on me. When he got over his nervous agitation, he behaved like a normal dog.

Despite the fits and starts, the frequent and frustrating runaways, there was hope.

XXVII.

A New School

On a typically cold and drippy winter morning in December, I put a long lead on Piki and let him and Blue out of the car at Fort Ebey for a walk. As usual, I looked and listened for signs of other people and animals. We hadn't gone far when two young men in sweats came from behind, overtook us, and jogged past.

I couldn't believe that I saw Piki suddenly speed up and lunge at the backside of one of them. The young man yelped and stopped on the spot.

Oh, my God! Had my dog just bitten someone? An unprovoked bite!

I'd seen it with my own eyes, but still I couldn't believe it. How could Piki do that when he was on a leash! I rushed up to the jogger, my words tumbling over each other. "Are you all right? I'm so sorry! I can't believe my dog did that."

"Well, here," the man said. He pulled down his sweat pants—he was wearing running shorts underneath—to show me a small but growing bruise on his thigh. "Now can you believe it?"

The skin wasn't broken or bleeding, but it looked like it had been severely pinched. The herd-dog nip.

I offered the man medical care and lots of sympathy, but he said, "No, no, I'm fine. It's getting better. He didn't hurt me. I'm okay."

He pulled up his pants and ran on, disappearing around a corner.

Too much time had elapsed to effectively scold Piki for the bite. He sat at the far end of the leash, abashed by the seriousness and intensity of my voice with the jogger.

This was serious. If this had happened when Piki was still in the shelter, he would have been euthanized. Let me explain.

WAIF has three reasons for ending animals' lives: if they have terminal diseases or injuries (believe it or not, people who feel unable to have their pet mercifully euthanized sometimes surrender them to shelters or dump them at large), or if they are known biters. The rationale is simple: these are not seen as animals that can live happily in people's homes as pets. In fact, there are many reasons for a dog to nip a human being. He might be succumbing to herding instincts, which is probably what happened with Piki and this jogger. Or the dog might be nervous and feel threatened. This came up at the WAIF shelter before visitors were restricted from touching the animals' cages. It happened several times that a person stuck his hands into a dog's cage and taunted the animal. If the dog had what would be, for a dog, a natural response—if he nipped that person—the dog paid with his life. He was put down.

That was not going to happen to Piki. I hadn't put in all this time and trouble only to let Piki be killed now. He wasn't in the shelter, but he simply couldn't be permitted to develop this habit.

Not only did I fear for Piki's life but also for the comfort and safety of any of the souls that he might sneak up on and attack.

These were people, not sheep, and Piki needed to know that biting them was unacceptable. I needed to put a stop to this, and fast.

We were scheduled soon to leave on another vacation. Piki would be boarded while we were gone. There was little else I could do now, and I didn't know where to begin when we came back.

Not long after our return, I was grocery shopping and over-heard a conversation in the produce department that steered us in a new direction. I didn't realize then, but it turned out to be the answer to my prayers.

Over the fruit and vegetables, a man and woman were *ooohing* and *aaahing* about what the trainer Clark Donahue had accomplished with dogs they knew. This surprised me. During my volunteer days at the shelter, I had heard about Donahue. He had a reputation for being physically extreme with dogs.

I had met Clark Donahue once about ten years before, when he offered to the WAIF board of directors the use of part of his property on Central Whidbey. I was one of a three-person team that went there to meet him and look over the facility.

Clark was a retired canine police officer. Besides offering beginning and advanced level obedience classes, he trained attack dogs. This is a no-nonsense task that is physically and mentally demanding and requires a mix of intimidation and profound gentleness. Clark dealt with animals whose roles switched every few hours. They'd go from being house pets to powerful, dangerous weapons and back again. Clark seemed to have those same pussycat/tiger qualities himself, but then he couldn't have been just an average, everyday person; not when he and his canine partner had, over years, counted upon one another to face dark, unknown dangers and emerge alive.

Clark and his wife, Monica, raised and trained their own pet Doberman Pinschers, several of whom, like furtive shadows, lurked on the perimeter of our walk around the property, watching their boss and keeping an eye on us.

Donahue's property was also cluttered with chickens, ducks, horses, and small livestock of various sorts, all of which scattered as we entered their territory.

As we walked around the property one of my team members and I made hopeful eye contact every time we saw something that might offer possibilities for WAIF. But he and I had little chance to compare notes at the time.

The other member of our team was a big city girl who never took on any work at the shelter that might dirty her clothes. She seemed to think those jobs were for other people. On this occasion I watched her flinch when she saw some maggots in a manure pile. I knew right away that Clark's services would be rejected. At the time, I wondered which of the women he would think put forward the veto—her or me. But I wasn't concerned; I figured I would never see him again.

When we were about to go, City Girl beamed and thanked Clark profusely, acting as if she couldn't wait to report the exciting and hopeful prospects to the rest of the WAIF directors.

Clark's personality that day was dominating, bigger than life. He was pleased with how the meeting was going. Expansive. In a deep, theatrical voice, he boomed that perhaps WAIF personnel ought to phone before the next time they came out to visit because his Dobermans would routinely greet any arriving car in the driveway. He laughed, "Don't even get out of the car on my property if you're not pure of heart."

I knew he was joking, but, somehow, this undertone of threat became my lasting impression of the day's events. All these years later, I had consciously chosen not to consider the Donahues when I first enrolled Piki in obedience school.

Now, it dawned on me that his reputation for being harsh with dogs probably came from his attack-dog work and from the very people who favored the no-corrections approach to obedience that had worked so poorly with Piki.

Anyway, I was desperate: I would have done anything to get control of Piki and this biting problem.

I phoned Clark and told him my name and Piki's problem.

"We need to do the basic on-lead training to teach him how to be properly corrected when he misbehaves. His biting will go away." Then, to my astonishment, he said, "Didn't I meet you at my house with some WAIF people a few years ago?"

"Yes." Still feeling guilt-by-association at WAIF's rude rejection of his long-ago offer, I brought our conversation back to my current need to obedience-train a semi-feral dog.

He obliged me. "Why, I've even obedience-trained a coyote!"

I was dumbfounded.

"Bring Piki to my house so I can size him up," Clark said. "Chances are good that I can do something for him."

Welcome words.

I drove up Clark's long, curving driveway off one of Central Whidbey's back roads and parked behind a line of cars next to a flat, open space like a small parade ground for working with dogs and horses. Monica was there, working with an obedience class of owners and their dogs. Clark strolled up the driveway and casually leaned against the car ahead of me.

I got out and walked to the rear of my car to remove Piki. I opened the door and Piki jumped out, cowering at the end of a short leash. Clark called me over to him at the other car. Piki followed me, straining to keep away from the unfamiliar man—tall, with dark hair and a deep voice. This was Piki's nemesis: anyone who looked like the man who had first brought him to the shelter as puppy.

"Just ignore him. Piki will soon be eating out of my hand," Clark said.

Without looking at Piki, he asked me if I was the one who had picked up an injured deer he had phoned the wildlife clinic about, not long after we first met.

I was. I was amazed at his memory of these two brief unrelated contacts.

Clark had found a young buck by the roadside. The deer had been hit by a car and was unable to move because of severe damage to his hips. Clark had put the deer into a large wheelbarrow, left him by the roadside, and phoned the wildlife clinic, which alerted me. I told Clark that I had called friends who lived in that area and asked them to meet me and help me with the deer. Together, my friends and I had immobilized it on my carrying board, loaded it in my car, and sang softly to comfort it as we brought it back to the animal hospital. Its prospects had been good.

From there, the subject turned to how much Clark admired the other WAIF lady, now deceased. He had never suspected—and I didn't tell him now—that she was the one who had recommended rejecting his services.

Piki couldn't move far on his short leash. He circled, sniffed, watched everything. Within a few minutes he gingerly moved toward Clark, first smelling his shoes, then his pant legs, ready to shy away at any movement. Clark continued to ignore him.

Like Piki, I began feeling more comfortable. I wanted to know how Clark had obedience-trained a coyote.

"Well, it was a young one that got hurt," he said. "Someone brought it to me . . . "

Excitement in my voice, I interrupted him: "Piki's actually touching you."

"Don't pay any attention to it. He's responding perfectly."

At that moment I saw Piki tentatively sniff Clark's cupped hand. The dog withdrew immediately, expecting a reaction. There was none. So he advanced again, this time nuzzling Clark's hand and happily pulling away with a small treat in his mouth. Still, absolutely no reaction from Clark.

It was hard for me to continue chatting. When I was able to speak, it was in a shrill, elated tone of voice.

Piki came back once more, took the last treat hidden in Clark's hand, and remained next to him long enough for Clark to stroke his head. Then Piki strolled to the end of his leash, delighted, licking his chops.

It was a huge leap forward, and it had happened so simply.

Part Five

Must Be a Show Dog

XXVIII.

Basic Training Again

March – May 2003

Our first obedience school hadn't worked for us. The subsequent agility classes had been only modestly effective. Some progress had been made when Piki voluntarily came back to me during the Thanksgiving Day runaway and the retractable leash incident. The invisible fence training and boarding at a kennel were encouraging Piki to come when called, but he still seemed to be different dogs on and off lead.

I wanted him to be *my* dog: to trust and obey me, to love me freely and without coercion, to do what I asked because he wanted to please me.

My great wish for Piki was that one day he would be able to run free, and that he would choose to come back to me when I asked.

To that end I enrolled us in Clark's next Basic Obedience class for beginners.

At the first lesson on a Saturday morning in early March, Clark greeted each handler in the driveway as we arrived. He instructed us to leave our dogs inside our parked cars, telling us they could enjoy a relaxing time-out in the car when it wasn't their turn to perform.

Clark led the eight student owners to a small tack barn near the driveway and the parade ground. He set out chairs and lit a fire in a small iron stove. It provided us a cozy talking-space to brief and de-brief.

Clark then began explaining his program, which taught corrections. He believed, as I do, that having discipline imposed from an external source builds internal self-discipline in any individual, no matter what their species.

His human students watched and listened intently as Clark revealed the mysteries of a choke chain. We were to administer it as a *zing pop*—a rapid, short tightening, followed by an instant release.

Since a dog is trained to heel on the handler's left side, a hold-over from predominantly right-handed gun-toting hunters, the chain links of the collar threaded back through the large 0 ring at the end to create a loop, should create the shape of the letter *p*, when it's on correctly—the loop of the *p* around the dog's neck and the stem of the *p* facing the handler. Set up in this direction, the chain loosens immediately when the handler releases pressure on the collar. If the collar is put on backward, in the *q* shape, the links do not release and the dog can choke.

We all practiced by slipping our choke chains up our legs to the thigh and quickly *zing-popping* so that we could each feel exactly what our dog would feel around his neck.

Clark inspected the leashes we'd brought and promptly deemed all of them wrong. He then cheerfully sold us each a six-foot short leash and a twenty-foot long leash with a thumb-loop at the human end, instead of the more traditional wrist-loop that the whole hand goes through.

"Enough control with just the thumb," he said, "and *more* than with the whole hand."

Clark stressed that the training of owner and dog was a cooperative effort, a working together and not a dominance issue. A dog works *with* its master, not *for* him.

He said that in a short time we would attach the choke chain with the twenty-foot lead on our dog, let the dog out of the car, and begin to walk away briskly. This was Clark's version of the *watch-me* lesson.

Predictably, at the end of the long line, the dogs would stop and sniff, or just wander off, not paying attention to the direction that the handler was heading. Ah, but when the tension increased on the lagging dog, it was the dog's end that had to give. The dog would receive a rude jerk while the owner continued walking, without slowing his pace. Because there would be a distance of twenty feet between them, the dog wouldn't associate the tug with the owner, who never would look back at him. The owner, in turn, could tell what was happening by feeling the line go slack or taut. The dog would sense that being jerked was his own fault and would rush to catch up, loosening the line. Feeling the line slacken, the owner was to sharply change direction and to continue changing directions until he felt the dog walking by his side.

One by one we took our dogs out of the cars while Clark supervised our execution of what he had directed us to do. True to his prediction, in two minutes or less each dog was trotting alongside the handler, looking up at the handler to learn in what direction they would be moving next.

If this was the extent of Clark's *rough physical treatment* that people in the community had whispered about, I knew it was something with which I could easily live.

After the *watch-me* segment, we began the *heel* command with our dogs. Over time this would include the basics of on-lead obedience training: sharp right and left-angle turns, diagonal left and right turns, left and right about-faces, doing full circles to the right and left, and doing figure-eights with people or objects acting as the end posts. Each time we stopped walking, the dog was required to instantly and automatically sit beside us. Clark quickly weaned Piki and some other dogs from sitting on the handler's left foot or leaning against them—looking for physical contact as a sign of approval. Piki learned to sit properly on his own weight, beside me, not touching me.

Clark's eagle eye observed every detail of both handler and dog whenever any pair performed alone, and it was the humans who bore the brunt of his corrections. He commented on us before talking about the dogs. Our posture, body language, and mannerisms reflected our confidence and control—or lack of it.

Over the next few weeks, the newly introduced lessons built on the basis of the old, constantly reviewed ones, adding *down, stay,* and finally, the most challenging of all, the *recall* or *come.*

When we worked in groups in the class, we were taught to keep our dogs away from the other dogs they were so eager to meet. In this way, we learned to control them.

Starting at the end of the second session, Clark asked everyone if they would be willing to stay a few extra minutes to do a drill especially designed for Pikachu. They were to put their dogs on a *sit-stay*, stand beside them, and act as human weave-poles. Piki, heeling at my side, and I were to briskly walk among them, weaving down the line, so close to them that we actually brushed against their bodies.

At first, Piki was terrified to rub up against all these strange humans, but as the weeks went by, he adjusted to it, just as he eventually adjusted to all the other fearful innovations in his life.

It was an extremely useful exercise, and I will be eternally grateful to Clark for recognizing Piki's special needs and addressing them.

When the dogs were not performing, either singly or in the group, they were relaxing inside their owners' cars. For Piki this was perfect. He became accustomed to making himself comfortable and receiving a treat at that time. In contrast, when he was outside the car and in unfamiliar territory, Piki was still anxious, still looking for a way out.

The whole training method, in addition to the off-duty car-lounging, was part of the system developed by Clark's dog training mentor, William R. Koehler, in his Obedience, Understanding, Training (OUT) program. Koehler had studied the effects of high-to-low-pitched sounds on dogs and discovered that the owner's barking a sharp, low-toned "Out!" to a dog instantly commanded its attention and respect, much more effectively than his saying "No!"

In the 1950s and 60s, Koehler became nationally known for his training of animals, many of whom starred in popular movies. Clark and Monica studied with Koehler in Southern California and modified his training to develop their own style of teaching dog obedience. Nowadays, some of Koehler's methods are regarded as being unnecessarily strong, but I never saw any indication of that in the way Clark worked with dogs in our class. He was never rough with them; he knew that Pikachu needed corrections, to be followed immediately by gentle touching as his reward.

My own behavior was proving as difficult to modify as my dog's. We were a month into the beginning class when I walked Piki late one foggy April afternoon in Fort Ebey State Park. We had walked for about twenty minutes when I looked at my watch: five o'clock. Time to turn around, go home, make supper and enjoy a quiet Saturday night. Piki had performed so well both on the walk and in class earlier that day, I thought I'd reward him by briefly letting him off-lead as we turned and headed back to the car.

He enjoyed his freedom. I enjoyed watching him luxuriate in it. That is, until we got back to within two hundred feet of the car. That's when Piki moved off the trail and into the brush, virtually saying, *I think I'll just stay here for the night. Come back for me another day.*

Damnation! Why had I taken the chance?

I called Piki to come. He didn't. I moved toward him. He moved away. I stood and waited. He lay down. When I moved toward him, he arose, warily. So, I stopped.

After a while, frustrated, angry, and hurt that he would betray my favor, I walked away and got into the car. He stayed where he was. I started it up and parked it closer to where he was.

Daylight was faint. An assistant ranger drove by and stopped to see what was going on. The park staff knew me well; we saw each other often. After listening to my problem, she drove on, closing one lane of the gate on the road and telling me how to close the rest when I drove out.

Darkness was falling when Curt drove up to the closed gate. He had come to find me. He was sympathetic. He understood both my frustration with Piki and my fear of leaving him—there are predators in this wooded park. Once Curt had verified that I was all right, he drove back home.

I looked at my watch: seven o'clock.

The dark forest loomed around me. I felt small, hungry, tired, and exasperated.

Finally, I decided to make a grand, noisy, and unmistakable show of leaving. I slammed the car door, started the ignition and drove slowly away, stopping nearby to close the park gate behind me, all the while watching constantly for Piki in the rear view mirror. I saw him rise from his mossy bed in the underbrush, follow the car at some distance behind, then climb the hill on the opposite side of the road. I parked the car, got out one more time, and called to him.

He came. His head hanging low and his slumping body language clearly showed he knew he had done wrong and I was not happy with him.

For a brief instant, I was relieved: the standoff was over. Then, anger overwhelmed me. It was a moment when I was tempted to give him a sound slap.

But he had come. And he shouldn't associate performing the correct behavior with a slap.

I counted to five, opened the car door without a word, and swiftly slammed it after Piki leaped in.

When I got home, I went straight to the phone to take advantage of the if-you-have-questions-call-anytime guarantee the Donahues had offered students. I called Clark.

"What should I have done?" I demanded.

"Exactly what you did," Clark said. "Walk away."

Piki graduated from Clark's Basic Obedience class in May 2003, scoring 189.5 out of 200 possible points on the final exam. I was pleased and proud. And relieved.

Still weak in the *sit-stay* and still nervous sitting next to other dogs with whom he had not officially performed the canine dominance dance, Piki had, nonetheless, passed.

This time, the change was truly taking place.

My feeling of pride at Piki's having overcome so many difficulties made me remember an important learning moment in my personal education. It was a response to a naïve question I had asked an older colleague when I started teaching years before. He had been carrying his physically handicapped teenaged son piggyback to a high school football game while his normal son walked alongside them and, watching them, I felt pity for all three. While making lunchtime conversation during the following week I asked the father, "Doesn't it wear you down to cope with a handicapped son compared to the normal one?"

His startled face slowly turned to a grin and he replied, "Just the other way around. It is so much *more* gratifying to have a child whose development is not taken for granted. You learn more. And you appreciate things you might otherwise not even notice. Those small successes, those rewards make up for all the difficulties."

XXIX.

Advanced Class Begins

June – July 2003

After a break of several weeks between classes, Pikachu and I launched into Advanced Obedience, the off-lead class taught by Monica Donahue.

I must admit I faced this class with a bit of trepidation. Monica, I knew, wasn't aware of this, but my uneasiness about working with her stemmed from two incidents that had happened during the Basic Obedience class with her husband.

During that class Monica usually worked with one of her horses at the far end of the parade ground about fifty yards away from our group, which was concentrated at the opposite end. Once when Piki and I were on the spot performing alone in front of Clark and the group, Monica had some kind of breakthrough with her horse. She shrieked, "LOOK, CLARK! I GOT HIM TO DO IT." Her loud, unexpected exuberance rattled me, distracting me and breaking my concentration when I was trying hard to focus. She did something similar when Piki and I were on the spot during our final exam. Neither of these interruptions was major and certainly neither was malicious, but I saw them as insensitive—and insensitivity was the last quality I wanted in a trainer for Piki.

Clark had always been encouraging to me and confident in working with Piki. With Monica I felt it would be a miracle if Piki did as he was told.

So, it was not with high confidence and enthusiasm that I entered the advanced session.

But I knew we *had* to do it. As he had shown with his refusal to get into the car on that April evening, Piki still had two distinct personalities: the good dog and the willful hound from hell. This off-lead training presented the greatest hope of fulfilling my goal for Piki: to become trustworthy. So, I bit the bullet and enrolled us in the class.

The first session was on a golden summer evening. The lowering sun glowed through the trees and wild shrubbery on the western side of the parade ground, emphasizing the fact that there was no fence between us and the forest—for Piki it would be an open-armed invitation to escape.

And this is where he was supposed to learn to go off lead?

Yes, but not immediately. Much groundwork was to be established before any of the dogs went off lead. That would happen weeks later in the course.

We resumed training on *heel* followed by the automatic *sit*, but with more clear emphasis on the owner's stepping out with his left foot at the same time he gave the command *heel*. This gave the dog both a verbal and visual signal to follow.

At the next session, the owner was required to step out on his right foot as he gave the dog the *stay* command and hand-signal.

There were to be no repeat commands. There was no room for *maybe he didn't hear me, maybe he was thinking about something else, maybe I didn't make it clear to him.* Each command was to be given once only with a swift *zing-pop* to follow if the dog didn't perform within a reasonably short time. If a dog broke a *stay* and tried to follow his owner, the owner was to rush back to the dog, pick up the dog's front legs, quickly walk him backward to the spot where he had broken the *stay*, plant him there, and walk away once again.

At the third class session, when we gave the commands *heel* and *stay,* we were instructed to whisper them, not to say them aloud. We were also careful to step out on the appropriate foot.

Between the classes and the daily repetitions at home, the dogs began to know whether they should *heel* and *stay* just from watching their owners' feet. At this point voice commands ceased altogether. This was a challenge Piki both enjoyed and met.

We continued to polish all our past work, in addition to adding new. We worked on *sit-stays* and *down-stays* with the dogs on the twenty-foot lead, the owner backing progressively farther away and requiring the dog to stay for a progressively longer time. Piki frequently broke the *sit-stay* because he was overly aware of the dogs sitting a few feet from him. It seemed to me I could feel Monica's piercing look skewer me as I ran to pick up Piki's front feet, back him up, and re-place him.

Over time, we perfected long line *recalls*, making sure the dogs trotted briskly to us and sat directly in front of us. Correcting the *recall* required only a quick, sharp jerk on the long line to initiate it. If the dog wavered from his direct path back to his owner, the owner was to reel in the line in large loops, bringing the dog to a sit directly at the owner's feet, facing him. Once the dog learned to come on *recall,* we practiced the *finish*, in which the dog learned to walk around from in front of the owner to the owner's left side and then to sit down.

When the dogs were comfortable with their owners being twenty feet away, we laid the long lines attached to their collars straight out on the ground between us and them and continued to back away, each time increasing the distance in small increments. By the time the owner stood more than twenty feet away from the dog, the dog was already in the habit of returning to him and finishing. Few corrections were needed.

We praised our dogs with words now, in addition to drawing small circles on their chests with our fingertips. The dogs were visibly pumped up about themselves when they performed well. They still enjoyed time-out breaks in the cars so they wouldn't become stressed by being constantly on duty. Several times during each class, the entire group of owners and their dogs went out on the parade ground and milled around, using short leashes and learning to encounter one another without the dogs interacting.

Monica added distractions to their tasks, carrying her cat out of the house and setting it down on the parade ground a few feet in front of six dogs on a five-minute *down-stay* with their owners standing forty feet away. Piki was well accustomed to cats, of course, and was not tempted. Other dogs ogled the cat with interest, but not a single dog broke its *stay*.

Told to find distractions on our own during the daily training between classes, I started taking Piki to the local shopping center. It was too hot during the summer to ask him to endure working on the blacktop parking lot, but we found a grassy park strip between the Wal-Mart parking lot and a nearby street. Cars driving by on either side were noticeable and scary. Piki rolled the whites of his eyes, but he learned to hold the *stay*.

We also practiced at the site of our almost-daily afternoon walk, Joseph Whidbey State Park. Out on the trail with Piki and Blue, I always required both dogs to come to *heel* as someone approached from the opposite direction to walk past us. We would go far enough off the trail to be out of reach of a dog on lead, then I would instruct both dogs to *sit* and *stay*. Many times I had to bark *leave it* to Piki as he reared up and tried to pull me to meet an approaching dog. Gradually, we anticipated this repeated procedure, and I told him in advance, "Now, I'm going to ask you to *leave it*, to *sit* and to *stay*." He began to anticipate what was expected of him.

Frequently, the person passing by would say, "Oh, what a good dog," or "I wish my dog was that good."

Hearing *good dog* from a total stranger made Piki feel very pleased with himself.

On these walks after he had enjoyed himself by smelling the smells and burning off some of his energy, we set to work in the picnic area practicing our homework, using the people who were there to serve as distractions. While Piki was on a long *sit-stay* or *down-stay*, Blue would greet friends or lay at a distance, watching. The same folks were often there at the same time of day and some of them who knew-us-when now began to marvel: "Is that the same dog?" "Is that Pikachu?" "That isn't the same dog you used to have, is it?"

Rabbits crept out from their walls of wild rose bushes and nibbled the grass a few feet away, winking at Piki and judging the distance they could safely run back when he broke his *stay* to charge them. I gave no repeat voice, hand, or whistle signals. Piki had learned he would only be told once. Though tempted, he stayed.

Around this time Piki also learned how to untangle himself when his feet got on the wrong side of his leash. I would command, *Fix it*, and he would stop, lift his feet so that they were on the proper side of the leash, and be ready to continue. Of course, he had dealt with this problem a lot because after his first escape he had dragged a rope for a long time and had taught himself to run with a gait like a pacer horse—placing his weight first on his right foreleg and hind leg, then on his left foreleg and hind leg—instead of at a trot, in which he was more likely to step on the rope or leash.

Piki also learned how to deal with stepping on something painful like a wild rose thorn. Then he would stop dead and plaintively look back at me with a *help-me* expression on his face. I would rush over, lift up each paw, and probe with my fingers until I'd found and extracted the cause of his owie. Grateful, he would continue on his way.

In order to experience a new location with different people and different distractions for our practice sessions, we sometimes went to City Beach. Everything there was close by—cars, strangers, new dogs—and there were different noises and smells, as well: all presenting new challenges to conquer. Piki did well.

It was there that I overheard several men who'd been watching us. One of them said to the other, "Must be a show dog or somethin'."

They couldn't have known that Piki was from the Pound. But, then, he didn't look much like his old shy and squirrelly Pound dog self anymore. Piki had a different presence, a different persona. He was more confident, more sophisticated—a dog of the world.

I smiled at the men and thanked them for their compliment. It made me look at Piki in a whole new way.

XXX.

The Light-Line

August 2003

About halfway through the advanced class, Monica introduced the use of a technique called the light-line, another Koehler brainstorm. We were to find a length of light, strong cord, tie a detachable metal hook on one end, and—taking pains to distract the dog so he wasn't aware of what we were doing—attach the hook to the d-ring on the dog's collar.

I went to the hardware store and bought a thirty-foot length of what we had called avalanche cord when I was a member of the ski patrol in Alaska years before. This light, woven nylon cord was strong enough to be used to support the weight of a person to hoist him off a chair lift if needed. The cord I bought was white, so I ran it through mud to subdue its eye-catching glare.

Early on, the dog was to wear the light-line whenever he was at leisure, inside or outside, so he would get used to its presence. Piki learned that he could romp, play, eat, and sleep with it on, and he stopped regarding it as a cumbersome foreign object. (It presented neither the rigid tension nor the noise that had so demoralized him when he was dragging around the detested retractable leash.) Though he was aware of the light-line around his feet, Piki had been used to dragging a line since he escaped from his first adoptive owner's yard. He already knew how to resolve getting tangled.

After the dogs had become accustomed to the light-line, we learned to go through all the various exercises of the class routine using the light-line in addition to the short or long leashes, depending upon the task. As Monica had instructed, each owner took great care to attach and detach the light-line discreetly, while distracting the dog with petting, treats, friends, other dogs—whatever was handy.

Then came the class when, with Piki sitting at my left side, Monica instructed me to make an obvious show of detaching the short leash, bunching it up in my right hand and tossing it away so that it landed several feet in front and to the right of the waiting, watching dog. Piki would clearly know the short leash was no longer attached. Then, with no voice command, but stepping out on my left foot, we immediately began a brisk *heel*.

There had been no advance warning that this would be the *ahah!* moment, but there it was—a sudden emotional rush of success, like seeing a child first ride a bicycle after its training wheels had been removed.

Pikachu and every other dog performed perfectly, as expected, their leashes lying behind them in the dust.

Later the same evening, quite matter-of-factly, we continued the *sit-stays* and *down-stays,* using only the light-line without the leash. The key to my always-shaky confidence about this skill was that, if Piki strayed or did anything else to make it necessary, I could step on the trailing light-line, either to halt him or to slow him down enough to pick up the line. Now when I stepped out on my right foot, signaling *stay* to him, I continued to run the light-line forward through my fingers, not to pull Piki but in order to string the line straight out on the ground in front of the dog, keeping it between me and him. That way, if I had to walk hurriedly back to correct Piki for breaking a *stay*, I could retain control of him by placing my feet directly on top of the line as I moved toward him.

During a briefing when all the dogs were resting in their cars, Monica introduced several new topics. First, she took orders from each of us for a custom-made tab: a one-inch diameter, five-inch long knotted rope with a hook that fit into the dog's collar. The handler could grasp it to control the dog, provided the dog was at close range. The tab sent a message to the dog that the owner still had the means to grab him, even though the dog was now off lead. These tabs were handmade by a friend of Monica's and, if we purchased one, it would be available at the next lesson. I chose a red tab, to match Piki's collar.

Second, Monica instructed us to think of a word, unique to each of us, that we could use as a release word for our dog: a cue to tell him that he was off-duty, at leisure, free to do what he wanted. It could be any word we pleased, except *OK*. She explained that *OK* was too common a word and might come up in a conversation we were having—and send the wrong message to the dog. The only release word I could think of that I would use exclusively in this context and not any other was the very word *release*.

She also instructed us to prepare a twenty-foot long line of light cotton kite string with a hook tied to one end.

Finally, Monica introduced the concept of the throw-chain. We were to gather the links of a choke chain with a piece of string—loosely but precisely so that the links would be noisy—and tie it with a knot. We carried this throw-chain tightly balled in our left hand to keep it from making noise until the right time and practiced tossing it at a target. The links separated in the air before they hit the target, and the throw-chain would land with a noisy clink.

Once mastered, the throw-chain was to be aimed to lightly hit a dog's butt, with the links clanking as they touched him. The point was to jolt the dog and propel him away from his owner at the same time the owner gave the *release* command. The key to success was that, like the surreptitious attaching and detaching of the light-line, the dog never associated the throw-chain with its master, never saw him touch it. The throw chain had to come out of nowhere to startle him.

Our homework would be to practice simultaneously using the throw-chain and giving the *release* command several times during the upcoming week while our dogs were on both the conventional twenty-foot lead and the light-line.

This particular class session was the high point so far in Piki's training. Unexpectedly, we had vaulted over the fear of failure and successfully used the light-line alone. All the long and tedious repetition that had prepared us for this point was suddenly—astonishingly—behind us and the goal of total off-lead performance loomed within sight. On this special summer night we drove the long way home, meandering northward on the side roads, savoring the sight of grazing deer, backlit by the setting sun in the still evening.

I stopped the car and, turning around in my seat, hugged Piki and whispered how proud of him I was. He leaned against me and licked the back of my head as I buried my face in his fur. I wanted him to know he had achieved something really special.

His ears plastered flat against his head, as they always were at his happiest, and his dancing hazel eyes showed that he already knew.

XXXI.

Success

In the few days before the next class, I practiced pitching the throw-chain left-handed, so I could maintain leash control with my right hand. I chose small target areas on a storage shed, a fence, a tree, tossing the chain to land lightly from different distances. As the chain hit the target, I firmly said *release*. The first impression this action made would be crucial: I didn't want to make any mistakes.

As time went by, my anxiety grew. Could I make this work? Would Piki respond as anticipated? Could I then retrieve the throw chain without his seeing me? Having the faith to actually try, that was the rub.

One day early the next week, on our afternoon walk at Joseph Whidbey Park, Piki was on both the twenty-foot lead and the long light-line, standing to my left and a few feet ahead of me. The time seemed right and I made up my mind to do it.

The pitch was perfect. Spread like a net thrown in the air, the chain lightly settled on Piki's rear end. I said *release* as he jolted ahead, startled.

I made nothing of it and let Piki go to the end of his long lead, gradually settling down to meander and enjoy himself again. After a short time, I put him on a long *sit-stay*. Instead of returning directly to him, I strolled around in a long half-circle and stood directly behind him for a while. Piki never turned to look at me, so it was easy to quietly bunch the chain, pick it up, and put it in my pocket. I walked back to my starting point and stood facing him from twenty feet away. When I said *come*, he trotted briskly to me, briefly sat facing me, and then moved to sit on my left side.

It had worked.

I was trembling with excitement. A few more successful tries at this and we would be ready to attempt it on the light-line alone. I was within a whisper of my goal to control Piki off lead.

Without a hitch, we completed the *release* and throw-chain combination on three more occasions before the next class. Each time we repeated the technique, Piki and I both became more comfortable with it.

At the beginning of the next class, each owner received the handmade tab to fasten to his dog's collar. Piki's braided red tab dangled from his neck down about five inches onto the white tuxedo-shirt of his chest. Its swaying and jiggling when he moved was something new to get used to, but it would be useful for me to be able to grab him, if necessary, when he was off-lead but still within reach.

We also changed our light-line from the nylon avalanche cord to the twenty-foot length of cotton kite string we'd been asked to get the week before. There were two reasons for this. First, we could wind this lighter cotton line into a smaller, tighter ball and carry it in our pockets. The second and key reason made my heart jump to my throat—Monica told us that she would cut a foot or more off the length of this light-line at each successive class.

That night she introduced an impressive new task: the *walking-recall*. I was to put Piki on a *sit-stay*, walk away with my back turned to him, and—without facing him again—turn my left shoulder and extend my arm to point back at him, bending the elbow quickly so that my arm came forward and swiftly letting it fall to my left side. The dog would stay until he saw the arm signal, then dash to catch up on my left side and come to *heel* as I continued to walk away. This cluster of commands was the *walking-recall*.

It took some doing to learn it. Monica modeled with her own Doberman. Ordering her dog to *sit* and *stay*, she massaged his chest with one hand, all the while fastening a light-line to his collar. Then she passed the light-line to a person standing about ten feet behind the dog. The dog didn't see Monica attach the light-line or give it to the person who held it. This light-line controlled the dog from breaking its *stay*.

Meanwhile, Monica also attached a long leash to the dog's collar, but let it hang loose as she turned her back and walked away from the dog, never putting any tension on it until she gave the new *recall* arm signal. Simultaneous with the arm signal, she put tension on the long line to jerk the dog forward to catch up with her as she walked. At the identical instant she gave the signal, the light-line holder behind the dog released that line.

At home, I enlisted Curt's help to hold and release the light-line as we practiced our homework between classes. It took Piki only three or four tries to master this latest challenge.

At last, we seemed to be a team, Piki and I, working together to anticipate, meet, and conquer obstacles.

One golden twilight, midway through the class, Monica told us to line up, shoulder to shoulder, with our dogs sitting to our left. While we were getting into position, she went away and came back carrying a large, no-nonsense pair of scissors.

Monica approached the line and, while the dogs remained at a *sit-stay* beside their owners, she singled us out, one by one, and told us to step out on a *heel* with our dog on the cotton light-line. Next, each owner and dog performed a series of figure-eight turns, followed by the dog doing a *sit-stay* about twenty feet from the line of other owners and dogs. Meanwhile, that dog's handler, after placing the dog in the *sit-stay,* turned his back to the dog, walked back to the group, and—turning to face the dog again—recalled him. The dog was to promptly return straight to his owner, sit in front of him, and then *finish* to a sit on the owner's left side.

After the first pair performed, Monica brandished her scissors and asked the owner to hand her his light-line.

Whack! Twelve inches gone.

The next pair didn't perform quite as well: only six inches were taken.

The next lost ten inches: not quite a full twelve.

Monica strode up to Piki and me, scissors in hand. As she nodded to me to begin, Piki nervously eyeballed her, but he moved out briskly as I silently began a *heel* on my left foot. Once we had moved a bit away from Monica, I noticed her sharp eyes assessing our performance.

I looked away: stick to the task at hand.

Piki faltered slightly on the *recall,* I think because Monica was standing close by my side. Instead of coming to sit directly in front of me, facing me squarely, Piki sat at a slight angle edging away from Monica.

Monica had never given Piki any slack in class. There were never any special exercises designed for him in the advanced class, as Clark had done with the beginners. No discernible understanding that Piki's unsocialized background might cause him to behave differently from any other dog. Piki had to measure up to her standards, and those were the standards she applied for all the dogs.

Standing there, before Monica and the rest of the class, I let myself imagine how humiliating it would be if she didn't cut off any of our light-line.

Whack!

Twelve inches of string dropped onto the grit of the parade ground.

I smiled, and Monica moved on to the next team of owner and dog.

The final exam was not far off.

On a mid-August evening, Piki passed the final examination, totally off lead. Though he wore the tab, I never had to touch it. As for the light-line, it had been slashed into oblivion during the remaining few classes.

The final exam actually proved to be almost a non-event. It was anti-climactic compared to the night that all the dogs had showed they could work on the light-line alone or the night Monica starting cutting the string. The sequence of skills that led to the dogs' going completely off lead was so effectively planned and administered that it was a foregone conclusion that all the dogs in this class would master it.

Piki's only weakness was, once again, being a little uneasy about the *sit-stay* next to other dogs whose rear-ends he had never had the opportunity to sniff. He scored in the high 180s out of 200 possible points.

I was so proud of him that I couldn't imagine I was making a mistake when I told Monica that I thought we could get an even better score on the final. I asked her when she would be giving it next. The answer was December.

Remembering how many weeks I had waited for her to make out the diploma for the beginners' class, I told myself that I might just as well wait until December for this diploma. I asked Monica's permission for Piki to repeat the final in December. Silently, I vowed to use the interim to practice so that he could do even better then.

XXXII.

Wag 'n' Walk

WAIF's annual Wag 'n' Walk approached. Remembering what a grand time Piki had had attending it the year before, I entered his story in the essay contest this year, as I had Blue's story the previous year:

PIKACHU

In Oak Harbor's busy City Beach Park one recent summer afternoon, my dog Pikachu and I were practicing our obedience lessons. As I walked away from him on a stand-for-examination command, I overheard two men watching us remark to one another, "Must be a show dog or somethin'."

I had to laugh to myself because Piki was as far removed from a pedigreed show dog as he could be: he was just about the essence of a Pound Dog. A good-hearted, short-haired, black-tuxedo mixed breed, he was probably born with some genetic wires crossed that caused him to be so shy and fearful of humans. In addition to that, he had likely been abused as a puppy, then unsocialized, and, through human carelessness, allowed to escape and run— fearful and unapproachable—in the woods of Central Whidbey for over five months of his first year. All of which resulted in making him a semi-feral dog, distrustful of men, women, and children, afraid of everyone and everything except other dogs.

And then I realized, He IS a show dog. He's an "I'll Show YOU" dog! I'll show YOU what a down-and-out Pound Dog really CAN do!

It's been a two-and-a half-year grind since I— with the help of my other dog, Blue, whom Piki trusted—succeeded in capturing him and bringing him back to his "home" at the WAIF shelter. Once back at the shelter, Piki had little hope of adoption because he made himself invisible to people who were potentially interested in him. So, to make a long story short, after a few more months he came home with me as a "foster-child," and we eventually adopted him.

Our friends thought we were crazy. We had never before faced a dog who had absolutely NO desire to please his humans, no concept whatever of "good dog/bad dog." Although my husband was kindly disposed toward him, if he even looked in Piki's direction, the dog would cringe and run to hide at the other end of the house. Totally unhousebroken, he was also a fear piddler. (It took well over a year before he no longer peed all over the veterinarian's floor.) Until the several months passed before he learned from Blue that he had to do his business outside and we could finally get the carpet professionally cleaned, we dared not invite friends inside our house. At any time of the day or night, I had to put a leash on Piki and take him outside. This continued for many months. It was becoming an "It's him or me!" situation with regard to marital bliss.

Piki wasn't the only slow learner in the family—I finally got appropriate fencing to confine him in our yard. Blue modeled behavior that I praised him for and Piki learned to copy it. He also learned the very positive power of touch and came to crave it. After a less-than-successful first attempt at basic obedience training, I found a different professional trainer who had faith in Piki's ability and desire to learn. This process finally cemented the bonding between dog and owner that I had experienced with previous dogs and found so lacking and unsatisfactory with this one.

Now, our friends are amazed at the happy transformation of our hopeless-shelter-dog-become-show-dog. And Piki has the paperwork to prove that he's an "I'll Show YOU dog": on August 12 Pikachu passed with flying colors the graduation exam for Advanced Off Lead Obedience.

Piki placed second in the contest and he and Blue both enjoyed attending their second Wag 'n' Walk. They reveled in the attention, strokes, treats, and kind words they received. Piki adored kibitzing with the other dogs and seemed more relaxed than ever to be around strange humans.

Once again, the prize was a free photograph by a professional photographer, this time a different person from the previous year.

The photo session, it turned out, was not a treat for Piki, He didn't like it when strangers tried to make direct eye contact with him, and he sure didn't like having a camera pointed directly at him.

The photographer began the session in his studio with a draped background, floodlights, and a camera fixed on a tripod. In order for this approach to work, the subject of the photograph had to be centered in front of the camera, unmoving, at the proper level, and looking at the camera. Piki stood, sat, and lay down, but he also squirmed, wiggled, tucked his tail, yawned almost constantly, and—most of all—he refused to make eye contact. His body language conveyed nothing but stress.

The photographer finally suggested that we move outside—maybe Piki would be more comfortable and relaxed. Piki did relax, but unfortunately, it was in the shade of a big tree, which altered the lighting conditions and gave the photographer fits. There, Piki lay down on his back, on his side, all the while keeping an eye on the young man with his now hand-held camera.

I decided that the photographer was going above and beyond the call of duty for a donated picture and called a halt to the ordeal. It was hard to say who was suffering more—the dog or the photographer.

Within a few days he emailed me a half-dozen pictures that he considered good enough to print. All portrayed an intensely alert, wary, and fearful subject. I selected one, had it matted and framed and hung it on my workroom wall under Blue's photo from the year before. It was not at all the same soft-edged, slightly blurred and dreamily suggestive pose. It showed a sharp-edged, bony and angular dog with piercing hazel eyes looking directly and quizzically into the camera lens. It was a very true likeness of Pikachu.

XXXIII.

Failure

December 2003

On a dark December night Piki retook the final exam. He was nervous and edgy from the moment we stepped out of the car.

We hadn't been on the Donahue property since our class ended in August. On that late summer evening, the sky had still been light. Now, at the same time on the clock, the sky was black and a clammy cold surrounded us. Unlike the established familiarity with the other dogs and people in our own class, all these dogs were new to Piki and, except for me and Monica, the people were new too.

Early on, I could see that retaking this exam under such different and increasingly stressful conditions was going to be harder for Piki, and I regretted the decision that I now recognized as an effort to boost my own ego by having him try to score better on the test.

Placed on a *sit-stay* between two big dogs that were strangers to him, Piki was jittery and uneasy. He broke the *stay*, and unbidden, ran the forty feet to me. I had to grab his two front feet and back him up to the place where I had originally placed him. This caused a further distraction for all the other dogs and upset the timing required to hold the *stay* for all of them. The same thing happened on the *down-stay*.

Within fifteen minutes, I knew we had failed.

When the group broke up, Piki gratefully leaped into our dark, cold car. Crushed, I got in with him, started the car, and turned it around. Even though he had passed the exam the first time, there would be no little piece of paper to say so now.

Monica was busy after the test, but she made the effort to come up to the car window and spoke to me briefly about using an electronic collar to correct Piki when he was off-lead and out of reach. She said she was looking forward to receiving one in the next few weeks as a Christmas gift, and she would be happy to offer it to me once she had mastered it.

On the drive home, I salved my disappointment at the failed exam with the thought that it made no difference whether or not Piki had an off-lead diploma. What mattered was that he'd gotten the training. I didn't have a trophy wall for my dogs. Proof of Piki's achievement wouldn't be on a piece of paper; it would be his performance with me, every day.

XXXIV.

At Last!

January – February 2004

The second exam showed that I could trust Piki to obediently perform off lead within a reasonable distance as long as he was not distracted by forces too strong for him to overcome, such as curiosity about unfamiliar dogs. We still had to settle the one remaining and very significant problem before my dream of letting Piki run free could be realized: he had to perform dependably at significant distances.

This is what Monica had been referring to when she proposed continuing with an electronic collar, an e-collar.

The invisible fence setup we already used to keep Piki within the boundaries of our yard involved the use of one type of e-collar, but I hesitated to move on to the field-training e-collar without knowing more about it.

Built into the invisible fence electronic collar itself is a small housing that contains a battery-powered receiver. It delivers a beeping sound for a few seconds when the dog comes within range of the transmitter wire buried underground. If the dog doesn't retreat from the wire, or if he actually crosses the wire, the beep changes to a shock. Two blunt metal prongs built into the collar deliver a moderate, but noticeable, shock to the front of the dog's neck.

A field-training e-collar differs from the invisible fence collar in that the dog's handler carries with him a small, portable transmitter. The dog will still feel the shock in its neck, but the strength is regulated by the handler when he pushes a button on the handheld transmitter.

Various manufacturers design collars with specific functions to suit specific purposes and a range of distances. Some models, designed to use with hunting dogs, can be used from as far away as a half-mile and can train a dog to pay attention to the handler's arm or whistle signals as an instruction of what action they want the dog to take or an intervention to prevent the animal from doing something wrong, even as a short, sharp correction if the dog does not perform a desired action.

Many people are reluctant to use e-collars because they don't trust their own ability to use the collar correctly and fear they will hurt their dog by delivering too long or too strong a shock. And some intentionally hurt their dogs by taking out their own anger on the animals.

Even though I was wary in my dealings with Monica, I knew her to be an excellent trainer and I wanted her guidance in using the field collar correctly. The first time I used it, Piki would already be loose and some distance away from me: if I did the wrong thing then, and it scared him, he could keep on running forever.

I wanted Monica to have plenty of time to play with her new Christmas toy and to master using the e-collar before we proceeded, so I waited to hear from her.

In mid January, I was walking the dogs one late afternoon when I ran into a friend whose Black Labrador rushed up to say hello. Mike, the Lab's owner, was carrying what looked like a small walkie-talkie in his hand and the dog's collar had a bulge in it.

"Hi, Shadow. How's my girl?" I bent over and scratched her back.

Shadow was a joy-digger, and she delightedly began excavating a huge hole in the sand while Mike and I chatted.

"Is that an electronic collar you're using?" I asked him.

"It is," Mike smiled and handed me the transmitter. "I've completely trained her to hunt off-lead by using it. It's waterproof and foolproof."

I was glad to hear it was waterproof because electricity and water don't mix, and you can't keep a Lab out of the water.

Mike showed me the model and brand he had chosen. It turned out that Shadow's collar had an additional button besides the one that transmitted the shock. The second button was small and red, and it transmitted a *beep* that was identical to the *beep* of our invisible fence at home.

When we had installed the invisible fence, I trained Piki to run away from it and toward me when he heard the *beep*. He had mistakenly crossed the wire once or twice, so he knew that a shock would soon follow that *beep*.

A slow smile spread over my face as the light dawned: Why couldn't I adapt that training to teach Piki to *come* when I beeped the e-collar? I could buy the same model as Mike's. I'd work with Piki on a long lead to teach him to come at the same instant I pressed the *beep* button. I might be able to avoid the shock button altogether, and I could hope to control him off lead as far as a half-mile away.

I verified this information by emailing an old friend in Alaska, a man who raised and trained bird dogs. He recommended the exact same model collar as Mike's and a dealer from whom I could buy it.

The collar was expensive, but seemed to be exactly the tool I needed to put the finishing touches on controlling Piki. Also, it was one that I could handle myself, without further obedience classes.

I hadn't heard a word from Monica since the night of the exam almost two months before. I knew she might just have forgotten her promise, but I didn't want to remind her and it was too frustrating to continue waiting.

I ordered my own collar.

By early February 2004, Piki was learning to come off lead to the *beep*—thanks to the training instructions that came with the collar. He responded correctly every time, so I hadn't needed to use the shock correction at all.

So far.

A daily walk was part of my husband's cardiac rehabilitation regimen following by-pass surgery several years before. Most mornings Curt walked Piki and Blue, and I took them in the afternoon.

Curt was uneasy about using the electronic collar, so he still walked Piki on the long lead. This seemed to work perfectly until one February morning when Curt and the dogs were deep in the forest on a trail popular with walkers, joggers, and bicyclists. Trusty old Blue trotted alongside, off lead.

When I heard Curt and the dogs return from their walk, I was working in the kitchen.

"Piki bit a lady," Curt announced without any prelude, his face ashen, as he entered the house. Blue and Piki burst in behind him.

My jaw dropped. I stood rooted to the spot.

"Where?"

"In the butt."

"No, no. I mean where did it happen?"

Curt sank into a dining room chair, not even taking off his hat, gloves, and jacket.

"We were walking on the Kettles Trail. Two ladies came off an adjoining trail and they were just a little ahead of us, going in the same direction."

"Didn't you have Piki on the long lead?"

"Yes, I did. I couldn't believe that he could do this while he was on-lead."

Neither could I. Except that he had done it once with me, nipping that jogger the previous year. "How did it happen?" I asked.

"Well, I don't know." Curt paused. "The women were talking, we were walking about fifteen feet behind them." He paused again. "I wasn't paying much attention because I had no idea he would do what he did."

"Did he just run on ahead of you?"

"Yeah," Curt paused, then squirmed in his chair visualizing the memory. "More like he sneaked up on them, now that I think about it. You know how he always has to smell everyone. I thought that's what he was doing."

"Did they see him? Did they stop?"

"No. They were really busy talking. If they saw him behind them, they didn't pay any attention to him. . . . Then I heard one lady yell, '*Ouch!*' They stopped and turned around. Piki slinked away from them and came back to me."

Curt said he had apologized then. He'd been as shocked as the woman who was bitten. He said, "I rushed up to see if she was really hurt."

"Was she?"

"She said that Piki'd nipped her in the butt. I couldn't very well ask to see the wound!"

We both laughed. Briefly.

"She laughed a little and said she was OK. What could I do? She wasn't mad at me or the dog, and she didn't seem hurt. She was very nice about it. After a minute she said she was all right. Then she and the gal with her kept right on walking and talking...."

Instantly resolved to right this wrong, I shot questions at Curt to determine the exact time and location of the incident.

That evening, I practiced giving the shock to myself at different strengths, wearing the collar around my leg. I found the right level of discomfort to make a lasting impression without doing lasting harm. Now, if I could just find the same ladies and recreate the situation, I was both prepared and determined to use the black shock button to correct Piki.

One time should do it.

The next day the dogs and I left home early to find the exact spot where the smaller trail joined the larger, more popular one. Then we hung around the area, and I hoped against hope that these women were daily exercisers and would appear there at the same time on this day. Piki was off-lead but wearing his electronic collar.

Soon, two women swung out of the small trail onto the main trail just ahead of us. They were walking briskly and so engrossed in talk that they noticed nothing else. I knew in my bones that this was the same twosome. Immediately, we started following them, keeping pace.

With a mixture of fear and approval, I watched Piki as he gradually closed on their backsides. They were so engrossed in conversation that they never saw him preparing to pounce on them, or me, simultaneously preparing to pounce on him.

A sharp cry of surprise rang out. But this time it came from the dog. He didn't know what had hit him and didn't associate me with the shock because I was some distance behind.

The women stopped and spun around, surprised to see the black dog retreating a few feet behind them, head down, tail between his legs.

I rushed up to them.

"Was it one of you that Piki nipped yesterday?"

They nodded. One of them said, "But he was with a man yesterday."

"My husband. He came home and told me about it. I was so hoping that I could find you today in order to correct my dog."

I explained how I had used the electronic collar from a distance because the dog simply *had* to know that he couldn't get away with this bad behavior. For them, it seemed to more than make up for yesterday's incident.

I apologized once again and added, "I don't think Piki will ever again sneak up on someone and bite them."

Then I pressed the transmitter's red button and beeped Piki. He sprinted directly to me.

We began what was, for me, a very satisfying return to the car. Piki and I were a team—and the final step was one I'd been able to take on my own. It was enormously gratifying.

XXXV.

Warm and Fuzzy

2004 – 2012

Piki became a vital member of our family: a loving, loyal, and obedient pet. No more running away. No more chewing shoes. No further use for a shock collar. Piki stopped leaving the room when my husband came in. He even started sleeping at the foot of our bed.

In 2005, four years after we adopted Piki, Blue passed away, and all three of the cats—Tessa, Halo, and Puck—died within two years of that time. This left Piki as an "only dog" for about a year, but in our family it wasn't a situation that could last for long.

Within the next few years two female orange tabby cats, Maize and Ginny, moved into our hearts and our home. Belle, a black mixed-breed dog—mostly herder—joined our family in 2007, when her owner had a stroke and could no longer take care of her. Belle and Piki became the best of friends.

To give an idea of how the small increments of intimacy developed in our everyday life over the next few years, I'll describe a typical day with this new brood of pets.

Just like all our previous dogs, Piki and Belle had what I call Alarm Clock Ears. When they wanted Curt and me to wake up in the morning, they'd vigorously shake their heads and set all their licenses and tags clattering and clanging like an alarm clock. This would be immediately followed by repeated sneezing and snorting in delight at being noticed. (As if it were possible *not* to notice them!)

Piki also developed his Great Getting Up Ritual. In a show of affection, he would run to greet me when I set my feet over the side of the bed or even just began to stir. He'd wiggle into a half-moon shape, begging for any loose hand to touch him. When I finally stood up, Piki would duck between my legs and maneuver me into position to scratch his waist, moving back to the sweet spot just in front of his tail.

We'd then walk down the hallway. I'd turn on the heat at the wall register, and we'd sit on the step between the kitchen and living room in our split-level home. At our house, this step is known as The Curb. I've always loved to sit on a curb, first on the street in front of the house I grew up in and now inside my own house. This inside Curb is right in front of a wall heater, and as soon as Maize would hear the heater start up, she'd rush to lie in front of it, tangling herself in the folds of my bathrobe. Stroking Maize would occupy my left hand, and Piki, leaning up against me, claimed my right side. I'd reach my right arm under his chest and up his right shoulder, drawing him to me. Belle would curl up next to Maize. For the moment I'd run out of hands, but Belle was still an integral part of our morning love cluster. These few moments of intimacy all four of us anticipated—no, required—to start the day off right.

The marvel for me is how much Piki himself wanted this special moment. I've loved other dogs and cats and shared special ritual moments with all of them, but I think this morning rite with Piki was sweeter, stronger because of our struggle to attain it. I had never been entirely sure that Piki would give up his love of being free among the tall trees to love being by my side in the house and garden. For a long time I didn't know that after walks in the forest and gallops on the beach, he'd choose to return to me. Sitting with him in the mornings let me feel the certainty of his trust and affection.

I'd then make breakfast for the dogs and cats, and Curt would make breakfast for himself and me. Toward the end of our meal, I'd loudly announce "Cleanup in aisle two." Hearing the spoon clank on the side of an almost-empty cereal bowl, Piki leaped forward, ready to perform his duty of licking the dish. The dogs then wandered away until I announced, without raising my voice or making any special fanfare, "Let's do teeth."

At that, Piki would skid onto the slippery vinyl kitchen floor first, beating Belle to the spot and dropping immediately to a *sit*. I squeezed chicken-flavored dog toothpaste onto a little red finger-brush; lifted first Piki's upper lip, then the lower lip; and ran the brush around his teeth and gums. He was delighted by this ritual, Belle less so. I think she agreed to it because Piki did.

Perhaps it was easier for Piki because he was more accustomed to having my hands inside his mouth.

At least twice a year, Piki suffered from an extremely upset stomach. I would recognize his distress immediately because he'd gobble grass in order to vomit and ease his digestive system. Our veterinarian taught me to administer Pepto Bismol by loading the pink liquid into a needle-less syringe, inserting the syringe into Piki's mouth, and gradually emptying the medicine into him. Unbelievably patient throughout this ordeal, Piki would sit on the kitchen floor as I repeated the process of pouring Pepto Bismol into him, creating a pink froth everywhere. Then we would deny him food and water for the remainder of the day and, by the next morning, he would have miraculously recovered.

Our day always revolved around our morning and late afternoon walks. Piki and Belle recognized all the signals, from the obvious to the subtle. I'd change from pajamas and a robe into street clothes. I'd run a brush through my hair and put on lipstick. Belle would leap up and be ready to perform when I asked her to go into the den to tell Curt we were leaving. I pushed the door ajar for her, and Belle would rush through, snuggle up to Curt's left side, wiggling. He'd be sitting at the computer. He'd laugh and run his fingers through her long hair: "Going for your walk, are you?" he'd say, smiling.

"See you in a bit," I'd call as I pushed the door shut. On many days there were a few other things I had to do then, disappointing the dogs' immediate expectations and briefly making them feel it had been a false start. But as soon as I grabbed my wristwatch from a shelf and a piece of jerky from a tin in the laundry room, they knew I was back on the right track.

When I finally sat down to put on my hiking boots, Piki would bound over, nestle his head on my lap, flop on the floor in front of my chair and roll over, eager for me to rub his belly with my stocking feet. This was the belly-up that years before I'd thought I might never get from him. I'd lean over him and gently drum his ribcage, singing nonsense syllables, and Belle would become impatient, barking her *woo-woo-woo: let's get a move on.*

I put on my jacket, looped the dog whistle over my head, buckled the dogs into their e-collars—a brief wrestle with Belle, an offered neck from Piki—and opened the door. The dogs would shoot through to the garage. Belle always leaped first onto the folded-down back seats of my car, dubbed by Curt "The HairMobile" for obvious reasons. Piki would hold back because, without any training from me, he had acquired the respectful habit of not entering until I said some phrase with the word *up* in it: *Mount up; alley oop;. okey, dokey, up you gokey; up, up and away.* Once he'd heard the right combination for that day, he leaped in.

Belle would sit behind the front passenger seat. Piki always stood or sat directly behind me while I drove, often resting the side of his head on my headrest, sometimes laying his head on my shoulder. His icy, wet nose would then nudge my hat off, followed by swipes of his warm, wet tongue. Within minutes, Piki would launch into his eager *are-we-there-yet?* metallic whine, nonstop and nagging, yet somehow performed without ever opening his mouth. Once in a while, he'd whack me upside the ear with his snout, as if he had told already me once to hurry and now I had better get going.

When we reached our destination and I parked the car, I'd open the rear door, saying, "Wait," while I touched the buttons on their collars to turn on the power. Then, at the magic word, "OK," I'd stand aside quickly because both dogs bounded out of the car in one giant leap.

The dogs then would perform a preliminary smell-check to find out what might be new since the last time they were at the beach. Piki would trot over to me, unbeckoned, and nudge me, as if to say: *See, I came to you. Treat, please.* Most of the time I could not resist this charming boy. He and Belle each got a small piece of jerky when we reached the far end of our walk and turned back, and again when they re-entered the car. Of course, they repeatedly begged for more and, when I was in the right mood, I issued treats in what I laughingly called our In-Flight Refueling Maneuver, which is to say never breaking stride as we walked.

Belle invited Piki to chase her by nipping him and coyly running away. Every now and then Piki would get irritated enough to seriously chase her, but most of the time, it was he who wanted Belle to chase him. They'd madly race around the beach, out into the shallow water, over the sand deltas.

Once they reached the slippery larger rocks and tangles of driftwood, I'd hold my breath. This was dangerous territory. Here, Belle would slow down and stop, looking wistfully after Piki who, sure-footed, zoomed through the hazards. When Piki returned to a safer area, Belle sometimes charged him again. Her chubby little body and short legs occasionally worked up enough speed to tag him, but most of the time, Piki outran and outfoxed her. Smiling and panting, the dogs would both splash into the water before we returned to the car.

Back at home, I'd work around the house, and the dogs would nap to recover from the morning walk. Piki barked at any daytime noise in the neighborhood: delivery trucks, garbage trucks, school buses, the mail carrier, kids arriving for piano lessons at the house to one side, and at the various young Navy men living in the house on the other side.

A couple of years ago, when our neighborhood was invaded by a family of peacocks, Piki took it upon himself to protect us from them. Hackles raised, barking, he would charge to the windows—Piki on the inside, the birds on the outside. This was an exhausting task as the peafowl voyeurs were both brazen and persistent, peeking in from the front door, the deck, the skylights, seeming to delight in teasing our cats and dogs and in violating our privacy.

When the afternoon was sunny and the backyard free from the temptation of peacocks and rabbits, Piki would flop down in one favorite place in the grass and sleep a long time, basking in the sun and sponging heat into his thin, black, racehorse body. When the weather was bad—which was more often—he'd back up against the wall heater at the foot of the indoor curb, stretch out next to it, and absorb all the heat he possibly could from that source. Some afternoons I offered to brush him. He'd trot from the lawn over to the deck and almost sink into a stupor, he did so love to be brushed.

On the other hand, he never became what you'd call a placid dog. Any sharp or unexpected noise continued to bother him: the occasional thunderstorms, fireworks, the doorbell; one of those infernal pizza delivery TV ads would make him go wild.

I would often have errands to run during the day and frequently left the house for hours at a time. The instant I closed my lipstick tube, Belle would be at my side, conveying an excited *Oh, goodie. We're going somewhere.* Both dogs would run eagerly to the door, only to be crestfallen when I delivered the eternal message: "You both be good. Piki, you're the dog-in-charge. I'll be back in a little while."

Once the dogs' body clocks announced it was time for the late afternoon walk, Piki and Belle would always descend upon Curt. As time went by, Curt could no longer walk comfortably, so he stopped his participation in our outdoor adventures. At this time of day he would sit in his recliner in the family room, reading. Piki, who had largely ignored Curt all the rest of the day, nudged Curt's right arm with his nose, forcing the arm up to form a hug around Piki's head. Meanwhile, Piki's tail thumped the chair. He rubbed up against Curt like a powerful and insistent cat, resting his nose on Curt's lap and demanding that Curt notice him and share his excitement.

Invariably, Curt would say, "You haven't paid any attention to me all day until now, and now you want me to notice you." Then his heart would melt, and he'd pet Piki and tell the dog that he loved him—forgetting any of the earlier turmoil that had existed between them. Both dogs wiggled and panted with eagerness to go, Belle *woo woo wooing*. This impressive display was designed to remind Curt that he would have to make their dog-dinners while we were gone.

Now and then I would take along a handful of pretzel sticks to snack on in the car as we drove away for the afternoon walk. Once, I put one in my mouth like a cigarette and absently turned my head to the right to speak to the dogs. Standing directly behind me, Piki snapped off the pretzel's other end. I laughed, and we did it again. It became a great game for us.

Both Piki and Belle became so accustomed to my saying "over here" or "on my left" that they would automatically run to my left side during our walks when I needed to control them in meeting other dogs or people. They would impressively *sit* and *stay*, and if I told them to *leave it*, they wouldn't break their *stay* to approach another dog. However, if the other dog and its owner were friendly and want to meet, then I let Belle break the *stay* first, followed by Piki.

After just the first few years, Piki would occasionally stop in his tracks if he needed help and he'd shoot me a distress signal. I'd tell him to *stay* as I hurried over to see what the trouble was. Often he would hold up a paw that hurt: he'd willingly stand still as I gently probed the pads and toes with my fingers. It was usually a wild rose thorn that I could pull out without any difficulty. Then his expression changed from one of anxiety to calm.

At times when grass Piki had grazed on the day before was still undigested in his feces and didn't exit with the rest of the poop, he would shoot me his embarrassed, *please-Mom-fix-it* look. Resigned to do a less-than-pleasant mom-task, I'd take a tissue out of my pocket and remove the grass while he stood, patient and grateful.

The only time that Piki was in real trouble, he rushed to me for help. We had been walking on the trail near the beach, and I'd let both dogs wander away across the driftwood line down to the water because there was no one else in sight. I heard furious barking and ran over to the water in time to see Piki turn-tail from two otters and head toward shore. All three critters were swimming some thirty yards offshore. I knew right away that Piki had chased the otters, thinking that he would play with them. They, however, viewed him not as a playmate but as a threat, and one of the otters attacked and bit him. A slight trail of blood diluted with seawater trickled down Piki's leg from his flank.

Once he was ashore, I parted his wet hair and examined the small wound. I hugged Piki like any mother comforting a child. The dog was trembling from fright and shock that his playful overtures had been so viciously rebuffed. He licked the wound and, after a few minutes, we turned for home, Piki limping slightly.

I phoned our vet as soon as we got inside the door. His office hours had already ended for the day, but he was still there.

We were both amazed at Piki's boldness. When we had talked enough to determine that Piki was not badly hurt, the vet told me to bring him into office the next day for an antibiotic shot. The next day, neither he nor I could find the wound. Piki was fine. After that, he kept his distance from otters, thank goodness.

On the way home from our afternoon walks, Piki would often lick the sweat off my neck and face as I drove. He'd rest his chin on my shoulder, and I'd loop my right hand around his head and neck.

Once we got back to the house, the dogs could barely wait for me to open the door from the garage. While we'd been gone, Curt had fed the cats and made dog dinners. Piki and Belle would rush straight to their bowls. Belle always ate slowly, but Piki gobbled his food — a lifelong habit from trying to compete with his littermates.

After standing aside at the door to avoid being trampled as we entered the house, Maize now sat on the kitchen floor with an expectant look on her face. The cat was waiting for me to take a can of aerosol whipped cream from the refrigerator. I shook the can and squirted a small dab on the vinyl floor for her and in their bowls for each of the dogs, who were happy to have this small luxury, too. *Let's Do Cream* was a holdover habit from the days when Tessa ruled.

One night after dinner many years ago, I heated up some left-over breakfast coffee and added a shot of Kahlua and a squirt of whipped cream. Tessa, who was sitting on the kitchen floor, was fascinated by this action, so I put a dab of cream on the floor for her. Delighted, she never let me forget it, and this became another family ritual.

Following dessert for the pets, I would move into the family room to join Curt. He'd have made a cocktail for me, and I'd sink into my recliner to watch the evening news. Ginny would have already curled on top of my chair's headrest. Maize would leap on top of the piano, circle, and bed down. As Curt and I nibbled on crackers or pretzels, Belle the Beggar would station herself on the dog pillow in front of the fireplace, staring hopefully at Curt, willing him to toss a treat to her.

Piki joined our evening coterie, sitting at the left arm of my chair, just inches away, his bright brown eyes fixed upon mine, entreating. I'd deny him for a while because I don't think giving dogs human food is good for them. But my handsome dog was irresistible: he had captured me and tamed me so completely that I'd offer him a pretzel stick.

Epilogue

On a bright early-June evening in 2012 I stumbled across two rawhide chew-bones in a cupboard and decided to give Piki and Belle a treat after their dinner. Musing about how many years had passed since they'd last had rawhides, I sent them into the backyard where they lay down, gnawing with pleasure.

A few days later Piki started his customary grass gobbling, and I knew that he was going to need his shots of Pepto-Bismol. He patiently endured them, but a day later he didn't seem any more comfortable. Usually he did. Wondering if he had fully digested the chew-bone and if I had done the wrong thing by giving rawhide to a twelve-and-a-half year old dog, I took him to the vet.

X-rays revealed a possible blocked intestine, and Piki spent the next two days in the animal hospital having barium tests and hourly x-rays. Finally, the vet sent him home, saying that the barium had passed without obstruction and Piki would be happier at home leading a normal life.

That Thursday evening when he returned, Piki strutted stiff-legged from the deck door into the backyard, barking loudly to announce to any animal within earshot, *I'm back and I'm in charge.* Belle, Maize, Ginny, Curt, and I all delighted in having him home and seeing him especially strong and assertive, happy to be back.

The next morning dawned dramatically dark and gloomy for the day after the summer solstice. The dogs and I went to a nearby park for our morning walk. In the low-hanging fog Piki wandered off the trail and stood in the tall, wet grass, staring into space. That's when I knew. It's just an inescapable feeling in the gut that this dog did not want to continue his life and I was doing him no favors by forcing him to live. Curt agreed.

The one thing that really bothered me was the question of whether I was putting an end to my beloved Piki's life for my own convenience. I was in charge of a major women's golf tournament to be held the following week. I was going to be very busy with that and wouldn't be at home and able to look after the dog. So, certainly it would not be convenient to have Piki be sick then.

But in spite of my guilt pangs, I still a strong feeling that the time had come to end Piki's life.

Somehow, we all made it through the rest of the day. In the late afternoon, we packed Piki into the back of the car with Curt in the passenger seat next to him, the two of them touching and comforting each other while I drove us to the vet's office. I wanted us to be the last appointment of the day and to not be waiting endlessly among a crowd of other pets and their owners.

Mercifully, the waiting room was empty, and the vet was not surprised at our return.

I held Piki in my arms on the operating table as the vet and his assistant prepared the shot. Just before Piki slumped and the vet announced that he was gone, I buried my head in Piki's and whispered in his ear, "Go find Blue."

Instead of crying uncontrollably, I felt strangely liberated. I had given Pikachu the very best I could. And after his rocky start, he'd had a happy life. I knew that. I had already written this book to memorialize him, so I knew that Pikachu would fade less from my memory than my other pets had, and that other people would have a chance to get to know him.

Thank goodness, I had the presence of mind to ask the vet to do a cursory autopsy. I had always accepted the inevitability of my pets' deaths before, but this time I just needed to know, if possible, what the cause of this illness had been. The vet was keeping Piki's body for cremation, and said that he would take the time over the weekend to see what he could find out.

On Sunday afternoon the vet phoned to say that Piki had terminal cancer of the small intestine and that the cancer had already metastasized. He said, "You did the right thing at the right time."

The timing was a great blessing for me as well. Instead of being paralyzed by grief, I was able to bury myself in the work of the golf tournament. When I received Piki's ashes, I stored them with those of Blue and Nacho, planning one day to have them mixed with Curt's and mine and scattered in a place we all loved to walk together.

Belle moved up from playing second fiddle to being concertmaster.

Just as I did, she desperately missed her buddy and saw Piki everywhere. Her eyes lit up and she wagged eagerly at any Lab we saw from a distance, always to be disappointed. She and I became very close over the next few months and it was a joy to do so, because I realized how obviously I had favored Piki over her. I was happy giving her the attention she deserved, and she finally settled into being *my* dog.

I seriously considered getting her an older canine companion, but hesitated because I have been being getting shots for dog and cat allergies for the last three years. Theoretically, I should let

Belle, Maize, and Ginny die off and not replace them. If I did, then my nose might stop running. In fact, my allergist would like it if I got rid of them sooner.

There is no question of doing that in my mind. Belle herself is pushing thirteen and, although her health appears to be okay, she won't last forever. I am, of course, fully aware that it is self-defeating to get allergy shots while sleeping with cats. Yet these animals are my babies, my children, my family, my support group. And one of the reasons I'm still in good health is the daily dog walking that I've done for so many years.

So, while I knew I wouldn't go out looking for a dog, if the right dog found me . . .

Acknowledgments

I offer my gratitude to my much-appreciated editor, Margaret Bendet, and to our mutual friend Dorothy Read for getting us together; to Ann Adams and Susan Mador for their helpful critiques of an earlier draft; to members of the Whidbey Writers Group, my cohorts, who patiently listened to my reading aloud the first draft, chapter by chapter, as it gradually became a book; to Tom Masters, who created the book's beautiful website www.runningfreethebook.com; to Darryl Newell, who greatly helped me with the photographs; to Gwen Samuelson of radio station KWPA, Coupeville, WA for her on-air support and for making available the recording of the radio reading of the "Over The Cliff" chapter to be included on the website; to Park Ranger Brett Bayne and map-maker Steven Ford for making possible the map of the Fort Ebey State Park hiking trails; to all the friends and fellow dog lovers who have encouraged me; and especially to my beloved husband Curt, who shared in both the work and the joys of reclaiming Pikachu, and without whose encouragement this book would never have taken form.

A Note on WAIF

Since its creation twenty-some years ago, I'm happy to say that the Whidbey Animals' Improvement Foundation has become a successful institution on Whidbey Island. It's so successful, in fact, that many people take for granted that WAIF has always existed and surmise that it is supported by the local and county governments. Some people complain the organization's policies and procedures are not sufficiently generous and that it does not offer every animal shelter service known to humanity.

I have my own opinion on the subject, and this very book is an expression of my gratitude for the work WAIF does.

WAIF is a non-profit organization registered in the state of Washington and is not affiliated with any other organization. Island County, which encompasses Whidbey and Camano islands, supplies funds to keep dogs during their mandatory first five days at the WAIF shelter, when it's hoped their owners will reclaim them. This same county largesse does not apply to cats, which are also housed by WAIF, and it does not support dogs between their fifth day of residency and their adoption. Island County does also provide a salary for an animal control officer, who works cooperatively with WAIF but is not directly associated with the organization.

What keeps WAIF afloat are community respect and support. Volunteers of all ages form the organization's backbone and donations—both financial and in-kind—are its life-blood. The money comes from bequests and from memorials, and it also comes from children—from kids who run bake sales and sporting events and raid their piggy banks, from Girl Scout troops and soccer clubs, and from birthday celebrants who ask their young friends to bring, instead of gifts, donations for WAIF. The community also donates all manner of furniture, and housewares, clothing and jewelry to sell for WAIF's benefit in the organization's thrift stores, one on Whidbey's North End and one on the South.

On Whidbey Island WAIF currently operates two animal shelters (in Coupeville and Oak Harbor) and two cat adoption centers (in Oak Harbor and Freeland). The organization is currently building a new shelter, virtually across the street from the existing one on the outskirts of Coupeville in Central Whidbey.

WAIF facilities are what is known as minimal-kill shelters. Of some thousand animals taken in by WAIF each year, less than 1 percent are euthanized—an extraordinarily low number. For the animals it serves, WAIF provides shelter, food, water, shots and other necessary medicines, bedding, cleaning services, supervised exercise, toys, laundry facilities, as well as the support of regular promotions and public events where adoptable animals are shown to the public. WAIF also spays or neuters every adopted animal before it leaves the shelter.

Such minimal-kill animal shelters have been increasing in numbers in the United States and worldwide, although many of the old-style "five days and out" facilities still exist and the numbers of animals euthanized by shelters is still appalling. These figures are not even dependable because there are in many such facilities no uniform standard of admission or recordkeeping policies, and statistics available online are not always current.

The Humane Society of the United States (HSUS) estimates that of the 6 to 8 million dogs and cats taken in by animal facilities in this country each year, between 3 and 4 million are euthanized. The American Society for the Prevention of Cruelty to Animals (ASPCA) puts those same figures at 5 to 7 million animals taken in and, again, 3 to 4 million euthanized. That is 60 percent of the dogs and 70 percent of the cats put to death—cats being the higher number of deaths because so few come in with identification.

Given these figures, WAIF's adoption rate is quite impressive.

A nationwide movement to promote *no-kill* shelters, as opposed to *minimal-kill* shelters, is presently taking hold, and WAIF has also been criticized by some who espouse that ideal. These no-kill shelters, however, often have strict standards of admission, accepting only healthy animals with good prospects for adoption. And since there are no commonly recognized standards among shelters, the accuracy and transparency of those records are always open to question.

WAIF takes in all strays and accepts surrenders of all companion animals except during times when it simply doesn't have space available. This has been known to happen occasionally during times of economic downturns and increased military deployments, when many are, sadly, forced to give up their pets, and during the annual late-spring/early summer kitten bloom that floods most shelters. At those times, WAIF provides a waiting list for surrendering pets.

Hopefully, public awareness of the humane treatment of animals will extend to more and more of those individuals willing to experience the ultimate joy of "doing the impossible"—reprieving the doomed by adopting them and learning to live with them happily. In this day, when the overbreeding of pedigreed dogs has led to intentionally mixed breeds—Labradoodles, Puggles, Cockapoos, and the like—the terms *hybrid* or *mixed breed* are a welcome change from the old-fashioned *mutt*. The large selection of mixed breeds at lower prices offered by your local shelter may include just the soul mate you're looking for.

Your experience of adopting and learning to love a shelter animal may, at times, be challenging for you both, but the tightness of trust achieved by surmounting problems together is worth the effort. Hopefully, it will be as rewarding for you as it was for Piki and my family.

www.waif.org

About the Author

It all started about forty years ago. Twice, while walking her dog on the beach in Anchorage, Alaska, Barb Bland found injured seagulls and took them to a local veterinarian to be treated. It was a satisfying experience and her first exposure to what became a calling for Barb: animal rescue.

Barb also volunteered with the ski patrol in South Central Alaska, doing human rescue, which is, she explains, much the same sort of thing: you search for individuals, immobilize them, and you haul them to safety.

Barb and her husband Curt were high school teachers in Alaska and though they lived in the city, the region itself was part of the frontier. "You knew that you couldn't depend on the powers-that-be to take care of everything that needed to be done," Barb says. "Even though you might not know precisely how to accomplish something, you learned to improvise."

Curt and Barb visited and fell in love with Whidbey Island, Washington in 1978, while involved in another high-risk challenge: crewing on a sailboat from Alaska, belonging to friends between Seward, Alaska and Victoria, British Columbia.

They took early retirement in 1980, moved to a property they'd bought on the north end of Whidbey, and proceeded to do all the things they had, as Barb puts it, "threatened to do while looking longingly out of classroom windows."

For Barb that meant learning to draw and use water-based art media, playing golf, gardening, traveling, and focusing on her family—which has almost always included some pet cats and dogs.

Soon after her arrival on Whidbey, Barb performed an errand-of-mercy for a neighbor, a single man whose beloved cat had died while he was deployed overseas with the Navy. The man asked Barb to dispose of the cat's bedding and dishes because he was reluctant to return to a house filled with painful associations. Barb found a wildlife rehabilitation group—a one family operation—that could put the cat's worldly possessions to good use, and she volunteered her own services as a driver.

Wildlife rehabilitation is now commonly practiced, but in the early 1980s it was a new endeavor and an adventure—yet for Barb it was the same search-immobilize-haul routine she knew so well. When the family left the area, Barb became one of the five founders of a state-licensed wildlife clinic on Whidbey Island. From there, she moved to the Whidbey Animals' Improvement Foundation (WAIF), which advocates and operates humane and minimal-kill animal shelters.

WAIF is currently building a new animal shelter on central Whidbey and most of the profit from *Running Free* is going to support the shelter's completion and maintenance.

In writing this book, Barb's intention is not to explain how to catch semi-feral dogs and adapt them to human households, but, rather to demonstrate the extraordinary rewards of working with these "problem" dogs and the commitment that's needed to do so successfully. "When people undertake helping a dog without considering the amount of effort it may take," she says, "they may end up becoming frustrated—and risk breaking the dog's heart as well as their own."